The Real Gypsy Guide to Fortune Telling

The Real Gypsy Guide to Fortune Telling

Deborah Durbin

Winchester, UK
Washington, USA

First published by Soul Rocks Books, 2015
Soul Rocks Books is an imprint of John Hunt Publishing Ltd., Laurel House, Station Approach,
Alresford, Hants, SO24 9JH, UK
office1@jhpbooks.net
www.johnhuntpublishing.com
www.soulrocks-books.com

For distributor details and how to order please visit the 'Ordering' section on our website.

Text copyright: Deborah Durbin 2014

ISBN: 978 1 78279 452 3
Library of Congress Control Number: 2014959935

A CIP catalogue record for this book is available from the British Library.

Design: Stuart Davies

Printed and bound by CPI Group (UK) Ltd, Croydon, CR0 4YY, UK

We operate a distinctive and ethical publishing philosophy in all
areas of our business, from our global network of authors to
production and worldwide distribution.

CONTENTS

Introduction

We all want answers to questions...

Although there is no specific date as to when fortune telling and divination first came about, historical evidence has shown that many different forms of fortune telling were practised in China, Egypt and Babylonia around 4000 BC. We're talking a long time ago here. A time when there was no Sky TV, iPads, cell phones or even electricity to power these things, so the only form of entertainment came from the telling of stories and predicting whether or not you would get eaten by a Tyrannosaurus Rex that week.

Throughout history, every human culture has had a need to question life, and all cultures across the world have developed their own way of answering these questions. There are literally hundreds of fortune-telling techniques that have been developed over the years, from astrology to tarot reading: the ancient Greeks would use astrology to predict future heroes. Medieval kings would call upon wizards to decide who they should marry and Romany gypsies have read people's fortune for years as a way of earning an income. Millions of people today, just like you, turn to fortune telling to help them with questions or problems they might have.

OK, so today it's more likely to be questions about whether you should take that job offer or whether the guy you're interested in will be at the party you're going to this weekend, but the basic principles are the same: we all want answers to questions.

This book will take the mystery out of fortune telling and give you an insight into how to use different divination/fortune-telling techniques, in a simple and safe way. This book covers everything from being able to give accurate Tarot card readings, to informing your friends of who to kiss, marry or avoid by using the art of numerology.

From The Author

This book is designed for anyone interested in learning about fortune telling to do so safely. Regardless of age, there is something for everyone here and you may find that you're drawn to just one or two subjects, or want to try all of them. Thanks to the good ole' film industry many think that anything to do with fortune telling is evil or to be wary of. That is just not true. I can assure you that there is nothing relating to black magic, devil worshipping, Ouija boards, or any hocus pocus within this book. All the fortune-telling techniques covered here derive from traditional Romany folklore, historical culture or are scientific based.

The great thing about being able to read fortunes is that whatever the problem, you will usually find a solution yourself. Fortune telling applies as much today as it did in the past. Wonder if that guy at work ignored you because deep down he really does like you and is just very, very shy? Wonder why your 'friend' has unfriended you on Facebook? Worried about your exams, starting a new job, or whether or not you should go to that party where you know your ex is going to be? Whatever the question, you'll soon be able to answer it.

Tarot Cards

Claims have been made for years that Tarot cards originated in China, India, and Egypt, but their true origin remains unknown. Traditional Tarot cards as we see in most films first appeared in Italy and France in the late 14th century. It is thought that Tarot cards were originally used for playing card games, but studies have shown that Romany gypsies have used them for the purpose of telling people's fortunes for years.

Today there are many different variations of the Tarot deck, from animals to astrology. Regardless of the design and packaging, all Tarot cards will follow the same principles. They all have a total of 78 cards – 22 Major cards (also known as the Major Arcana) and 56 Minor cards (also known as the Minor Arcana). The Major cards are the ones of most importance when doing a reading. They are the ones that you should take notice of because they signal big things happening in your life.

The Minor cards are also known as 'suit cards'. Like a regular pack of playing cards, the Minor cards have four suits: Wands, Swords, Cups and Pentacles. Each suit has ten numbered cards, plus four court cards (king, queen, page and knight), and represent the more minor or practical day-to-day things and emotions going on in your life.

Have a read through the following information on Tarot cards and see if you can remember what each one means by looking at the key notes that I have included. If you can get hold of a pack of Tarot cards to study, even better. If you can't, you can make your own, which I will show you how to do at the end of this section.

We're going to look at the 22 Major cards first…

THE MAJOR ARCANA

The Major Arcana are not associated with the suit cards (Minor cards). They are answers in their own right and although you will often get Minor cards within a reading, they support any Major cards that you draw.

All Major cards are picture cards, which often give you a clue as to their meaning. They are numbered from zero through to 21 and represent important and big things happening in your life. Listed below are the 22 Major Arcana cards from a traditional Tarot deck and what they mean.

THE FOOL

The Fool card is the first card in the Major Arcana and is often illustrated as a jester who is about to step off a cliff. This doesn't mean you should too, nor does it mean that you should avoid walking near cliff edges, although it does make sense not to. In medieval times, the fool or jester was someone who was a bit of a rule breaker, someone who stood out from the crowd.

You are being reminded that it's OK to be unique – in fact uniqueness is a very good thing. You will be full of ideas and this card tells you to take chances, be brave and be spontaneous. If that guy still hasn't asked you out, why not make the first move? It might not be the kind of thing you would normally do, but what have you got to lose?

The Fool also tells you to believe in yourself and your abilities. It pays to remember that the majority of other people all have hang ups too. They may have six billion Facebook friends or millions of Twitter followers, but deep down they have insecurities just like you. The Fool is telling you that by making a stand and taking chances, you will be the one to reap the rewards.

Key Notes:
New beginnings. Starting something new. Going on a journey.

Be impulsive. Have faith. Stand out from the crowd. Follow your dreams.

THE MAGICIAN

The Magician is a literally a magical card in the Major Arcana and is one of the most powerful cards you can draw. This card tells you that you have magic at your disposal and can use this powerful force to achieve great things.

The Magician is usually depicted as, well, as a magician. It symbolises the magic that is all around us, all of the time. The problem is, not that many people believe it's there.

By magic I don't mean the type of magic you see in *Vampire Diaries* or *Harry Potter*. I mean those times when things happen in your life, as if by magic. For example; you could be worrying about an up-and-coming exam and suddenly something just clicks into place and you realise that you do know the answers to the questions, or you're desperate for some extra cash to buy those fabulous shoes and you receive some money in the post from your aunt.

By drawing this card it's telling you that you have the power to do anything you want to. Yes, really. By tradition, the Magician is not afraid to act. He takes risks and focuses on what he wants. This is the message to do the same: focus on what you really want and you'll find a way to get it. Without sounding too 'out there', you only get one shot at life, so why not be the best you can be?

Key Notes:
Power. As if by magic. Follow your dreams. Take risks. Chances. Opportunities. Take action. Make an impact.

THE HIGH PRIESTESS

The High Priestess card is a bit like having a big sister looking out for you, (without all the arguments, borrowing of clothes and fights that usually come with having a big sister) and is said to be the guardian of your conscious.

The High Priestess is a bit like having all your female idols rolled in to one. If you think about all the girls and women you would love to hang out with for the day, the High Priestess is just this. She's sassy, independent, kind, caring, fun and knows what she wants in life. When you draw this card it's telling you that you too can be all of these things and that you are being looked after. Get a bit of self-confidence back and you'll soon see that people look at you in a different light.

You don't have to put up with feeling like second best. You're just as important as anyone else out there. If you think that everyone else is having the time of their lives, has more friends than you do, looks better than you do, and is more popular than you are, well, guess what? They're thinking the same things. Really, they are. You'd be surprised at how many other people are worrying about exactly the same things as you are.

The High Priestess is a message to tell you to stop worrying about pleasing everyone and just be yourself.

Key Notes:
Confidence. Sister. Looked after. Imagination. Power. Hidden talents. Believe in yourself. Be different. Be the real you.

THE EMPRESS

The Empress is another guidance card and again refers to a female in your life, often a mother figure. This could be your mum, a big sister, an aunt, a neighbour or a friend who is always on hand with a cappuccino and a box of tissues to offer sensible advice.

The Empress is also the card of fun and is telling you to not take life too seriously. So often we are told that we should do this or that; we should study harder, we should think about our futures, etc. This is often good advice and the people offering it usually only have our best interests in mind. Sometimes, though, isn't it enough to just live and have some fun? If you spend your whole life with your head down, planning for your future, you tend to forget that the hours, days, weeks, you've been doing this, you've missed out on actually living and enjoying the day-to-day things, such as the sun coming out for an hour, or a great song on the radio.

The Empress is reminding you that whilst we can't spend every day dancing on the beach, we can stop what we're doing and have a bit of fun every day. Choosing this card encourages you to indulge in what you enjoy doing. If you discover what it is you love most doing in the world and you can work out how to turn that into a career, you will never have to really work a day in your life, because it will never seem like work to you.

On a more practical level, this card also tells of riches coming your way. This could be in the form of extra cash, a present or even just a new lippy.

Key Notes:
Dance. Embrace today. Live. Fun. Laughter. Presents. Guidance. Motherly figure. Saying no to convention. Living for today.

THE EMPEROR

The Emperor card looks like a stern father figure, sitting on a throne. This is some sort of authority figure in your life. It could be your dad, an older brother or a teacher who commands respect, but who is firm but fair. This person will soon help you out in some way.

This fella is the organiser of the Tarot pack and likes every-thing to be in order. The message here is to get organised. Clear out your room and get rid of all the stuff that is just taking up space. This doesn't just apply to material stuff; it can also be a sign to let go of people who are no longer helping you. If your best friend of ten years no longer calls you, or is always too busy doing other things to meet for a coffee, let her get on with it and make room for new people to come into your life. If your boyfriend is into his football more than he is you, show him the red card and make room for a new attentive guy to sweep you off your feet.

There's no denying, when you pick this card, changes are ahead for you, which at first might feel uncomfortable, but you'll look back and realise that the changes are necessary for you to move forward.

Key notes:
Father figure. Help from someone. Changes. Let go. New people. New opportunities.

THE HEIEROPHANT

The Hierophant is someone who is described as a holy man and is often depicted in sets of Tarot cards as a priest. In fact, this is a person who holds secret knowledge and is someone you can turn to in times of trouble who will offer you words of wisdom.

These words might not make sense at first, but you can be assured that they will do, eventually. If you've been having a hard time recently or have been wondering whether you're on the right path or not, look for someone (a teacher or mentor) you can trust who will listen, who will not judge and who will offer you advice.

Sometimes by just drawing this card you are being told that a higher power, (such as angels) is looking out for and after you. If you can remember one thing, remember that everything that happens, be it good or bad, eventually becomes history. However bad things may feel, you are being told that it will soon be in the past and that bigger and better things are on the horizon.

On a more practical level, this card indicates new groups and friends coming into your life.

Key notes:
Mentor. Teacher. Help. New friends. Groups. Angels.
Protection.

THE LOVERS

The Lovers card is not just about whether that guy is really in love with you or not. It has several meanings. The image on a set of Tarot cards is usually of a couple holding hands or in an embrace.

The Lovers is often seen as a card of emotions and is a positive sign that those in your life, or coming into your life, love you for who you are. Being a Major card, this is an excellent card to draw, particularly if the question you have asked is about love. It's a happy card and one that gives you a 'yes' answer to a question. Relationships will blossom and will be happy and full of fun and laughter. If you're wondering whether you should go out with a certain person, this card is giving you the green light to go for it.

If the question you ask is about things other than relationships, such as should you go to college, apply for a particular job, or will you pass your driving test, this card is effectively saying 'yes' to you.

This card also means choice between two people. If you are unsure of who you should choose, look at the other supporting cards in your reading.

Key notes:
Love. Passion. Choice. Relationships. Yes. Positive. Emotions.

THE CHARIOT

The Chariot card is usually illustrated with a Roman chariot or cart, being driven by an Emperor-type figure. This is a card of power and a great one if you are looking for a positive response to a question.

The Chariot is a sign of victory and success, so if your question concerns whether a situation will have a good outcome – for example, will you do well in your exams – by drawing this card you are being told, yes.

Another meaning of this card is of being in control of your own emotions. You do have choices in your life. Just as the chariot horses would run wild if the driver didn't control them, it's up to you to make the right choices for yourself and your life. It's only you who has control of your own life and how you feel at any given time.

Some people have endless problems thrown at them, and yet they remain positive that things will eventually work out. Others wallow in self-pity because they're having a bad hair day. There is only one person who can decide whether your mood is bad or good on any particular day and that person is YOU.

In many Tarot decks, the word *Abracadabra* is written across the chariot. It means things will happen as if by magic – but only if you remain positive. Anything is possible now and you are in control at all times.

Key notes:
Control. Luck. Ambition. Success. Victory. Emotions. Magic.

STRENGTH

In traditional gypsy cards, the Strength card is usually shown as someone fighting a lion, but this card isn't about physical strength or telling you to go to the gym four times a week for a good old cardiovascular workout. This card is reminding you that you do have the strength to get what you want out of life, regardless of what obstacles you might be up against.

For example, you may be going through a tough time at school, college or work, you may find you're the target of bullies, or your boyfriend is being difficult, or you're just not getting on with your family. If you pick the Strength card, it's a way of telling you not to worry. Take a step back and look at the situation from an outsider's point of view. I've always had a philosophy that whatever life throws at me, it's never (thankfully) been a life-or-death situation and that it will pass and I will cope.

Whatever the problem, you *will* have the strength to cope with it. Often things are not as bad as they first appear. When you draw this card you can be assured that you do have strength on your side and you will win through this.

Key notes:
Strength. Victory. Challenges. Obstacles. Free from worry.

THE HERMIT

The Hermit card is usually illustrated with a person standing alone and the message here is one of withdrawing from things for a while. This doesn't mean it's giving you permission to lie in bed for three weeks, refusing to wash or brush your teeth – that's just disgusting. It's telling you to retreat from those who sap your energy on a regular basis, or constantly use you as a sounding board.

This equally applies to social networks. Whilst Facebook and Twitter are a fantastic way to keep in touch with what everyone is up to, it is very easy to get suckered in to living a virtual world and very easy to get caught up with what's going on in other people's lives and believe that they are all having a way better time than you, when in fact they are just like you. They too have insecurities and hang ups.

By picking this card, it's reminding you to take some time out. Often the Hermit turns up when a relationship comes to an end. When this happens, our instinct is often to go out and find another someone to replace the person we're no longer with. This card is telling you not to do that. Enjoy your own company, do the things you like and enjoy your friends.

On a more spiritual level, the Hermit is telling you that when you switch off from the outside world, the answers you are looking for will suddenly come to you.

Key notes:
Quiet time. Withdrawing. Silence. Time out. Own company.

THE WHEEL OF FORTUNE

This is a great card to turn up in a reading. It's usually depicted as, yes, you guessed it, a wheel, but is sometimes shown as a sundial on some decks of cards.

The Wheel of Fortune is a positive energy card and assures you that as with everything in life, things change. If you've had a run of bad luck, if nothing seems to be going right, then things are about to change for the better for you.

Everything happens in cycles – hence the wheel in the Wheel of Fortune card. When things are down, the only way they can go is back up. Sometimes we have to experience the crappy stuff in order to make way for the good stuff to come into our lives. We also have to experience things in life that result in negative experiences so that we don't repeat mistakes and learn from them. For example; if you put your trust into someone who abuses that trust, you learn not to be so trusting the next time.

The main message in this card is telling you that things are on the up, there is light at the end of the tunnel now, and you are about to have a brighter future.

Key notes:
Good fortune. Good luck. Positive energy. Bright future.

JUSTICE

The Justice card is usually illustrated by a judge, dressed in a gown, sitting on a chair, but it doesn't necessarily mean that you are going to be up before the courts!

Justice in the Tarot means that if you've been wronged by someone, they will be found out and 'justice will prevail'. We've all come across someone who is rude or unfriendly or tries to get one over on us. When you pick the Justice card, it's telling you not to worry, that the person will soon reveal themselves for what they really are.

The Justice card is the most basic of the laws of Karma, which shows that all actions will be returned eventually. If you're a kind person and try to be kind to others, you will receive kindness back in return. If on the other hand you bully people, or are unkind to others, well, yep, you will eventually get the same treatment back. You get back what you create for yourself.

When this card comes up in a reading it's assuring you that if you've been the victim of injustice, if someone has been mean to you or you've been accused of something that you haven't done, the truth will come out soon.

Key notes:
Justice. Battles won. Karma. Pay back. Victory.

THE HANGED MAN

The Hanged Man is based on a mythological figure called Odin who was said to hang by his foot from a tree to earn knowledge. Whilst there are far easier ways to gain knowledge than hanging around a tree, the message here is one of patience.

Many people believe that like the Death card, the Hanged Man card is a bad omen. None of the cards in a Tarot deck are 'bad'. As with any form of divination, they are merely tools that tap into your subconscious and guide you.

The Hanged Man card means that you may need to 'hang around' for a while, until you get an answer to something. This could be waiting around to hear your exam results, waiting to hear whether you got the job, or waiting to hear from someone who promised they would call.

If you study the Hanged Man in a set of cards, he's not suffering. He's usually just hanging around, smiling. He knows that there is no point in getting cross or impatient because the answer he needs will come eventually. You just need to be patient right now. Enjoy the moment of waiting with anticipation. Smile, knowing that whatever you're waiting for will soon come.

Key notes:
Patience. Waiting. Hanging around. Tolerance.

DEATH

The number of times I've heard, 'Oh, crap, the Death card. We're all gonna die!' whenever the Death card is drawn. First and foremost let's get one thing clear, the Death card DOES NOT MEAN ANYONE IS GOING TO DIE! And yes, I AM SHOUTING!

It doesn't help that many Tarot decks illustrate this card with either a skeleton or a cloaked man, holding a scythe aloft as though he's an extra from a horror movie!

The Death card is one of regeneration or rebirth. By that I don't mean birth as in having babies. It means positive change happening in your life. This might not appear positive at first. It could be news that you suddenly have to move house, leaving your friends behind, or it could be that you're being made redundant from the job that you love, or saying goodbye to a relationship. It may feel as though things are out of your control and you have no choice in the matter.

For us to grow and experience life, we need change. We need to move on sometimes to allow us to live a better life, meet new people and do new things. It may feel a bit scary at first, but it is necessary for us to grow and the Death card is always a positive change.

Key notes:
Changes. Positive news. Fear of the unknown. Excitement.

Transformation.

TEMPERANCE

If you study the Temperance card in a deck of Tarot cards, you will notice that the woman pouring liquid gold from one vessel to another is doing so with a smile on her face. This is because she is self-assured and knows that everything will be OK and she won't spill a drop.

The message here is telling you that all is fine in your life, or if you've been having problems, they will soon be resolved. This card is all about balance, so if you've been overdoing it recently, it's telling you to take a deep breath and go and do something relaxing. You may have been under pressure with studying or exams, or you may have had a lot on at work or school. It will all be worth it and the Temperance is a sign that everything will now run smoothly.

The Temperance is also an indication of a committed relationship. This could be a new friendship or a romance. Whatever it is, it's a good sign that this person will be in your life for a while and may well turn out to be your soul mate.

Key notes:
Harmony. Good things. Soul mate. Friendship. Balance. All good.

THE DEVIL

This is another one of those cards that is misunderstood and I do wish they would change the titles of some of these cards!

The illustration of the Devil card is usually, err...a devil! This little chap often has his arms and legs chained up. This doesn't mean that you will suddenly develop a passion for bondage, or will find yourself chained to the bedpost. The real meaning of the Devil card is one of constriction.

This could come in various forms: for example; you may have

to wait patiently for exam results to come through before you can go any further with your education. You might have to wait for that certain someone to call you before you can move on. You may have to endure another year at college, or stay in your job a while longer before you can go travelling. The message is that things will happen, but you will need to exert a little patience before you can finally get there.

This card also represents being temporarily tied down to something. You might have to abide by the rules of someone else until you can break free on your own. Remember, you're not being punished, it's just that sometimes the best things really are worth waiting for and they will come.

Key notes:
Patience. Constrictions. Tied down. Temporary. Tolerance.

THE TOWER

This is the third card in a pack of Tarot cards that is often taken the wrong way. Some will tell you that by drawing this card, it spells doom and gloom to come. This is not true. Whilst the illustration of the Tower card does usually look a bit depressing, with its building on fire and falling down, it doesn't mean that your house is going to burn down any time soon!

The real meaning behind the Tower is of change and like the Death card, the change is always positive, although it will feel far from it at the time. An example of this is, if someone has fallen into the habit of expecting another person to do everything for them and suddenly they are left to fend for themselves. This could be moving away to uni or having to start a job for the first time. The shock will jolt the person into taking responsibility for themselves, rather than relying on someone else to sort it all out for them all the time. At the time it feels as though the person's world is tumbling down on top of them, but in the long run, they are always thankful for the change.

As we grow up, there are tons of changes we have to cope with and yes, they are scary and we would much rather stay under the duvet than do them, but if we all did that and all stayed the same, nothing would ever move forward in our lives.

Think of any major changes as positive challenges.

Key notes:
Dramatic change. Scary. Positive. Growth.

THE STAR

Finally! One of those cards that is just busting with positive news! The Star card is a fabulous card to pick in any reading because it signifies everything that is good in your life and has a warm, snuggly glow about it!

When you draw the Star card, you can be assured of great things. On occasions it can literally mean that you are going to be a star, so get that application for the X-Factor filled out! If warbling for a living isn't your thing, then by drawing the Star card, it's telling you that you are about to 'shine like a star'.

Whatever your question might be, this card is telling you that miracles are about to happen. I'm not talking about that Jesus guy turning water into wine, although that's pretty impressive. What is going on here is that whatever you wish for in life, it is about to happen. You've heard the saying, 'wish upon a star', well this card is telling you that your wishes are about to come true.

This is a great card to have in any reading because it tells you that things are about to go supernova for you!

Key notes:
Stardom. Miracles. Shine. Good things. Wishes come true.

THE MOON

The Moon card is one of those cards that can have many

meanings. It can be seen as both a positive and a negative in some respects. I'm sure you've all heard about the effects of the moon – some humans are very affected by a full moon and the word lunacy comes from the Latin word 'luna', meaning moon. Studies into the moon and its effects on humans have shown that hospital admissions and criminal activity increase during the period of a full moon.

When you draw the Moon card it is telling you that not everything is as it seems. Other cards will clarify which area you are dealing with. Interestingly I have found that whenever I've drawn the Moon card, there has been a period of about six weeks before the truth is revealed.

There could be someone in your life that is not to be trusted, or you could be deceived by someone. Often this card appears when you are at a crossroads in your life; unsure of which path to take next. The message is to not do anything drastic right now. Allow the next few weeks to develop and then everything will become clearer.

Key Notes:
Deception. Six weeks. Trust. Withhold decisions. Wait.

THE SUN

This is another one of those fabulous cards that is great to receive in a reading. The illustrations on this card usually show a huge, bright sun, with children and animals playing in the background, flowers in bloom and generally all round good fun.

That is the message of this card. Life is to be lived and enjoyed and by drawing this card you can expect great times ahead for you. This refers to whatever question you have asked the cards. So, if for example you are asking about whether your love life will improve, the answer is well and truly YES! If you are worried that a friend has stopped talking to you and you don't know why, you can be assured that it will all be resolved very soon.

The Sun card is one of those cards that override any negative cards. If you do a reading where there are a lot of negative cards in there, but you have the Sun card mixed in, then the problems or worries the more negative cards show will not really be much to worry about. This is a great card to have at the end of a reading because it shows that things are about to get better for you.

Key Notes:
Joy. Hope. Success. Love. On the up. Happy times.

JUDGEMENT

The Judgement card means just that – that you are going to be judged in some way. It's a card of new beginnings and often turns up in a reading when the questioner is about to start something new – a new school, moving up to college, moving house, a new relationship, a new job etc.

We are all victims to judgement. How many times have you seen someone in the street and automatically judged them on the way they look? As much as I'd like to say we're above that, we all do it to some extent, so it's no surprise that you will be judged too.

First impressions are lasting impressions and I always advise people to show their most positive self to the outside world. If you're going to be judged anyway, you might just as well be judged in a positive light.

This card also highlights leaving the past behind. Today is a new day and as long as you are alive, you can always start afresh. The Judgement card can also signal you doing the judging. Just as I'm sure you don't like to feel as though you're being judged, this is a reminder not to judge people until you really know what they are like.

Key Notes:
Judgement. Critic. Changes. Leave the past behind.

THE WORLD

The World card is a lovely card to draw in any reading because it's reminding you that anything is possible and that the world really is in your hands.

It's a very positive card and tells that whatever obstacles have been in your way, you can jump over them, leave them behind and move on now. It's also the card of the traveller, so you could soon be on the move, but it will be a conscious move, not one that is forced on you.

The World card marks an important turning point in your life and I've often seen it come up when people are coming to the end of one thing and are ready to move on to another more exciting life. This could be leaving college and starting your first job to leaving your job to literally travel around the world.

This card also indicates a promotion or a life that you have always dreamed about.

Key Notes:
Travel. Journey. Reaching your goals. Moving on. Exciting times.

Now we have covered the Major Arcana we will look at the Minor cards, otherwise known as the suit cards. These are the supporting cards to the Major cards and deal with our emotions and feelings in general. Although the Minor cards are not as important as the Major cards in a reading, they provide us with information about how the person is feeling at the moment and can quash any worries that the questioner has regarding different matters.

As with playing cards, there are four suits in the Minor cards – Swords, Cups, Coins and Wands. There are 14 cards in each suit. The suit cards can be read upright or reversed, depending on which way they come out of the pack.

THE WANDS

The suit of Wands is associated with a spiritual level of consciousness and emotions. They highlight what is important to you. They are the cards that show what makes us tick. They are also day-to-day cards and what we do on a daily basis. If a reading is made up of a lot of Wand cards, it shows that the person is looking for answers in their life.

One/Ace of Wands
Upright: New beginnings. New Projects. Opportunities. Love. Creativity.
Reversed: Lack of motivation. Feeling bogged down.

Two of Wands
Upright: Planning your future. Decisions to be made.
Reversed: Fear. Not sure what to do.

Three of Wands
Upright: New enterprise. Progress. Expansion.
Reversed: Delays. Obstacles. Challenges.

Four of Wands:
Upright: Celebration. Marriage. Home life.
Reversed: Miscommunication. Change of lifestyle.

Five of Wands:
Upright: Arguments. Tension. Conflict.
Reversed: The same as upright, but worse.

Six of Wands:
Upright: Victory. Awards. Prizes. Progress.
Reversed: Lack of confidence.

Seven of Wands:
Upright: Competition. Persevere. Challenges.
Reversed: Challenges. Overprotective.

Eight of Wands:
Upright: Action. Movement. Change.
Reversed: Delays. Obstacles.

Nine of Wands:
Upright: Have faith. Test of courage.
Reversed: Paranoia. Defensive.

Ten of Wands:
Upright: Responsibility. Hard work. Success.
Reversed: Avoiding responsibility. Stress.

Page of Wands:
Upright: Free spirit. Discovery. Exploring.
Reversed: No direction. Stuck in a rut.

Knight of Wands:
Upright: Energy. Action. Impulsive. News coming.
Reversed: Frustration. Delays.

Queen of Wands:
Upright: Warm woman. Determination.
Reversed: Demanding. Shy and quiet.

King of Wands:
Upright: Leader. Business man. Entrepreneur.
Reversed: Ruthless man.

THE SWORDS
The suit of Swords deal with emotional and spiritual

development and often have double meanings, both positive and negative. They highlight the pros and cons of a situation and look at both sides of the story. Primarily they deal with people's emotions and the physical aspects of life in general.

One/Ace of Swords
Upright: Justice. Victory. Winning of arguments.
Reversed: Obstacles. Arguments. Losses.

Two of Swords:
Upright: Balance restored. Good energy. Good choices.
Reversed: Deception. Trust issues. Bad choices.

Three of Swords:
Upright: Temporary separation. Upheaval. Moving on.
Reversed: Permanent separation. Plans go awry.

Four of Swords:
Upright: Peace. Order. Everything is OK.
Reversed: Chaos. Bad timing. Testing times.

Five of Swords:
Upright: Limitations. Fear. Insecurities.
Reversed: Dangerous situation. Move on. Defeat.

Six of Swords:
Upright: Travel. Changes at work. Stress-free time.
Reversed: Obstacles. Boredom. Stagnation.

Seven of Swords:
Upright: Cunning plan. Foresight. Problems solved.
Reversed: Plans go awry. Check travel plans again.

Eight of Swords:
Upright: Lack of confidence. Restrictions. Progress.
Reversed: Negativity. Indecision. Feeling trapped.

Nine of Swords:
Upright: Courage. Isolation. Activity.
Reversed: Sadness. Difficulties. Loss.

Ten of Swords:
Upright: Rebirth. Start afresh. New beginnings.
Reversed: Let go. Be honest. Self-respect.

Page of Swords
Upright: A young person. Independent. Unpredictable. A message.
Reversed: Dishonest youngster. Business matters need looking in to.

Knight of Swords:
Upright: Career-minded person. Skilled. Passionate.
Reversed: Defensive. Difficult situation. Conflict.

Queen of Swords:
Upright: A strong woman. Support. Good friend.
Reversed: A bad friend. Struggles. Caution.

King of Swords:
Upright: A father figure. Man who will help you. A lawyer.
Reversed: An awkward man. Unfriendly. Government official.

THE COINS

The suit of Coins deal with the material world in which we live and primarily with money and prosperity. Interestingly enough, the higher a Coin card, the more money will come to you. This suit also deals with business matters and career achievements. They give you an idea of what your financial aspects in life will be like.

Ace/One of Coins:
Upright: Gifts. Money coming. Luxury.
Reversed: Greed. Overconfident. Obnoxious.

Two of Coins:
Upright: Financial changes. Move of house. Motivation.
Reversed: Emotional instability. Confusion.

Three of Coins:
Upright: Training. College. Work rewards.
Reversed: Expansion. Loss. Hard work.

Four of Coins:
Upright: Financial stability. Inheritance. Business.
Reversed: Low self-esteem. Loneliness. Worries.

Five of Coins:
Upright: Friendships. Faith in oneself. New start.
Reversed: Loss of friendship. Loss of faith. Loneliness.

Six of Coins:
Upright: Entertainment. Theatre. Spiritual.
Reversed: Confusion. Selfishness. Loss of faith.

Seven of Coins:
Upright: Completion. New projects. Good news.
Reversed: Delays. Hard work. Decisions to be made.

Eight of Coins:
Upright: Talent. Energy. More money.
Reversed: Lack of direction. Laziness.

Nine of Coins:
Upright: Independence. Cash coming. Material wealth.
Reversed: Work problems. Delays.

Ten of Coins:
Upright: Generous wealth. A new home. Settled life.
Reversed: Ties. Burdens. Delays.

Page of Coins:
Upright: A young person. New ideas. Scholarship. Ambition. Messages of good news.
Reversed: Wasted talent. Laziness. Snobbery.

Knight of Coins:
Upright: A young man. New friends. Patience needed.
Reversed: Errors. Mistakes. Stagnation.

Queen of Coins:
Upright: An independent woman. Advice given. Creativity.
Reversed: Insecurities. Materialistic. Untrusting.

King of Coins:
Upright: An older man. Advice. Money on its way.
Reversed: An older man. Impatience. Materialistic. Mean with money.

THE CUPS

The suit of Cups deal with our emotions, primarily love and all that goes with it. They highlight our dreams and the things that really matter to us, such as family and friends. They are generally happy cards and show what our wishes are (the nine of Cups is considered to be the wishing card). They give you an idea of what your dreams and desires in life will be like.
Ace/One of Cups:

Upright: Love affair. New romance. Motherhood.
Reversed: Artistic. Creative. Production.

Two of Cups:
Upright: Permanent bond. Soul mates. Engagement.
Reversed: Rivalry. Conflict. Parting.

Three of Cups:
Upright: Emotional growth. Psychic abilities. Fulfilment.
Reversed: Victory. Waiting. Patience.

Four of Cups:
Upright: New directions. Change of career. Changes ahead.
Reversed: End of a relationship. New romance. Advice.

Five of Cups:
Upright: New beginnings. New path. Inheritance.
Reversed: Heirloom. Ignorance. Greed.

Six of Cups:
Upright: News. Ambition. Fruition.
Reversed: Nostalgia. Living in the past.

Seven of Cups:
Upright: Right choices. Creativity. Rewards.
Reversed: Warnings. Concentrate on one thing at a time.

Eight of Cups:
Upright: Happiness after sadness. Maturity. Peace.
Reversed: Leaving a place behind. Artistic endeavours.

Nine of Cups:
Upright: Wishes come true. Emotional fulfilment. Kindness.
Reversed: Wishes come true. Overindulgence. Contentment.

Ten of Cups:
Upright: Lasting happiness. Fame. Success.
Reversed: Property matters. Contracts. Success.

Jack of Cups:
Upright: Artistic. Young person. Messages. Birth of a child.
Reversed: Major changes. News coming. Messages.

Knight of Cups:
Upright: Young man. Emotional. Intelligent.
Reversed: Invitations. A trip. News on its way.

Queen of Cups:
Upright: Romantic woman. Sensitive. New horizons.
Reversed: Moodiness. Self-deception. False romance.

King of Cups:
Upright: Powerful man. Professional. Lawyer or doctor. Warm hearted.
Reversed: Sensitive man. Crafty. Self-indulgence.

If you don't have a pack of Tarot cards...

If you don't have a pack of Tarot cards to hand, or can't get hold of one. You can make your own. You will need some good-quality white card to cut out 78 blank card shapes from. Try to cut them all the same size, because they will be easier to handle. Separate 22 cards to make your Major cards. Use colouring pens/ pencils/stickers etc. to illustrate each card as per the Major Arcana. If you are not particularly artistic, you can find images on the internet and stick them on instead. Do the same with all the Minor suit cards. You can laminate each card to make the deck last longer if you want.

Whether you buy or make your own deck of cards, shuffle them thoroughly and leave them out on a window sill when there is the next full moon, to charge the cards.

How to Read the Tarot Cards...

Tarot cards are a tool to tap into your subconscious. You could say that we already know the answers to the questions we have, which in some respect is true. Our ancestors would trust their instincts whenever they had an important decision to make. These days we are so busy in our daily lives that we seem to have forgotten to trust ourselves. When we use tools such as Tarot cards, we can tap back into that intuition. I'd love to be able to tell you why tools such as the Tarot cards work, but unfortunately I can't. All I do know is that they do have an uncanny way of predicting the outcomes of questions we want answering.

Shuffle... `

The most important thing to do before you do a reading is to shuffle the cards every time you use them. If you don't, you will often find that cards repeat themselves in a reading because the cards haven't been shuffled properly. If you are doing a reading for someone else, ask them to shuffle the cards.

Deal...

There are many, many spreads out there that you can do with Tarot cards, but I always find that the best ones and most accurate are the ones where you think of a number, divisible by three and count that amount of cards out.

For a quick past, present and future spread, you count out three, obviously. But for a more in-depth reading, count six, nine or twelve cards out and then one extra as the outcome card.

All readings start from left to right and from the first card through to the last. The first card highlights what has recently happened to you and the last card highlights what the future holds regarding a specific question. The very last outcome card will give you an overall look at the answer to the question.

Below is an example of a six-card reading for a question about whether Emma should go out with Adam:

Card one: Knight of Coins:
This indicates that the question is about a young man, under the age of 35. He loves nature and animals and is a little bit flirty.

Card two: Four of Wands:
This card shows that Emma is a happy person and that marriage and commitment is important to her.

Card three: Strength:
This is a Major card which shows that Emma is a strong person and usually gets what she wants in life. If she goes out with Adam, the relationship will be a strong and good one.

Card Four: Seven of Cups:
If Emma hooks up with Adam, the relationship will last and will be a happy one. It will bring emotional rewards for both of them.

Card Five: The Hanged Man:
If Emma doesn't make the first move, she could be waiting a while for Adam to do so. She may have other commitments at the moment before she feels she can embark on a relationship.

Card six: The Knight of Wands:
Adam is highlighted here as a charming young man who has lots of energy and is impulsive.

Card seven: The outcome card: Two of Cups:
This is the outcome card which shows that if Emma decides to go out with Adam, it will be a happy and long-lasting relationship. They could easily be soul mates. Given that all the cards drawn in this reading are positive, this in an indication that yes, Emma

should go out with Adam.

Due to the limited space here, it is impossible to show you every spread, but you will find the spreads that you design yourself, will have more impact to a reading. If for example you wanted to see what the year ahead has in store for you, you could do a 12-month reading, picking out a different card for each month of the year. If you wanted to ask the cards if your relationship is heading in the right direction, you could chose six cards, which is the number of the Lovers card in the Tarot. If you want to know about your career, choose nine cards to give you an overall view on what is happening. The important thing when reading the cards is to trust your instincts. If the Strength card turns up in a reading, say for example, if you were asking a question about your love life, it doesn't necessarily mean physical strength. It could be telling you that your inner strength will be important in the relationship.

Play around with different spreads for different questions and always trust your intuition when you read a spread. Obviously if a spread shows lots of negative cards, it will be a good indication that all is not well in the person's world right now, but take note of how many cards are emotion (suit) cards and how many are Major cards, because the negativity could be coming from how the person is feeling right now, rather than by circumstances.

Tea/Coffee Readings

Whether you are a tea drinker or prefer going to Starbucks for your morning latte, this section will show you how your daily caffeine fix can predict what's coming up in your life. This section will demonstrate how to do both tea and coffee readings, with common tea leaf and coffee bean symbols and their meanings.

TEA-LEAF READINGS

Tasseography, or tea-leaf reading as it is more commonly known, is an ancient Chinese practice that spread to Europe with the nomadic gypsies around the mid 1800s and is thought to have originated in Asia, the Middle East and Ancient Greece. The name derives from the Arabic word of *tassa*, meaning cup and the Greek *graphology* and *mancy* meaning divination.

The term also refers to the reading of coffee grounds and this is a very much favoured pastime and tradition of the Middle East. In France, tasseography is often applied using the sediments of wine.

Although it is often commonly associated with gypsy fortune tellers, the traditions of tasseography can be found in many different cultures. Modern tasseography is still very popular and is taken very seriously in Scotland, Ireland and Eastern European cultures. Philosophers believe that this is due to the constant human desire for understanding the self and the need for answers.

Just as the studies of the human mind grew during Victorian times, tasseography quickly became a popular parlour game during these times. However, the art of reading tea-leaves separates itself from many other fortune-telling techniques and magic tricks in that it is considered, much like the art of the Tarot, to be an effective tool for tapping into the subconscious in order to decipher the meanings of the symbols that appear to the reader.

Just as different cultures have different views on the same subject, the art of tasseography is no exception. Instructions such as how you should prepare for your reading, even down to how many times you should spin the cup vary from country to country. For example; in some cultures it is ill-advised for anyone to attempt to read the tea-leaves using tea from a modern teabag. In others they say you can't read your own cuppa, but as with any divination tool, I feel that you can use whatever means you feel like.

Whilst it is a rare thing to find a practising tea-leaf reader today, let alone a genuine tea-leaf reading gypsy, it is still an interesting and uncannily accurate form of divination and with a little practise you will soon be able to read your own and other people's tea cups. It can be fiddly and requires patience when you first start, but it is also a great game to play on a girls' night in!

What you need to read tea-leaves:

In days gone by people didn't have teabags and tea was sold loose. You can still buy loose tea today and most supermarkets will sell it. It's always best to use a fine grain tea if you can because the leaves will stick better to the cup. If you can't find loose tea, you can always split a teabag and use the contents. The second item that you will need for a successful tea-leaf reading is a white or pastel-coloured teacup. It needs to be a light colour otherwise you won't be able to see the leaves inside. The cup you use should also have a wide brim so that the leaves have a greater chance of sticking to the bottom and sides of the cup.

Additional items that you will need are a wide saucer upon which to place your teacup, a teaspoon for stirring the tea and a teapot. The teapot should be a china or porcelain, rather than metal. You can now buy teapots and teacups specifically designed for fortune-telling purposes.

Preparation

Boil a kettle of water. Once the water has boiled ask whoever you are doing the reading for to throw a small handful of the tea-leaves into the teapot and then ask them to give it a stir. Wait a minute or so to give the tea chance to brew. Next, pour the tea into the cup and allow it to cool – do not add milk to the cup.

When the tea is at room temperature ask your volunteer to concentrate on a question or an issue they wish to resolve. Even if the person you're reading for doesn't like tea, ask them to take a few sips.

Reading the tea-leaves

When you feel ready take the cup in your most dominant hand and turn it three times in a clockwise direction – make sure that you cover the top with your other hand to prevent any spillages. Next, pour any remaining liquid from the cup down the sink. Place the cup upside down on the saucer and once again turn it in a clockwise direction three times. Now you can look into the cup. You should notice that the leaves will be clumped together in different places inside the cup, including the rim, the side and the bottom. You are now ready to read the tea-leaves.

Symbols

As you turn the cup around you will notice shapes emerge in the form of the tea-leaves. Below is a list of common shapes and their meanings.

A

Abbey - Freedom from worry.
Ace of Clubs - A letter.
Ace of Diamonds - A present.
Ace of Hearts - Happiness.
Ace of Spades - A large building.
Acorn Success - Financial success.

Aircraft - Sudden journey.

Alligator - An accident.

Anchor - Success in business and romance.

Angel - Good news.

Ankle - Instability.

Ant - Success through perseverance.

Anvil - Conscientious effort.

Apple - Business achievement.

Arc - Ill health, accidents.

Arch - Journey abroad, a wedding.

Arrow - Bad news.

Axe - Difficulties and troubles that will be overcome.

B

Bat - False friends.

Bath - Disappointment.

Bayonet - A minor accident.

Beans - Poverty.

Bear - A journey.

Bed - Inertia.

Bee - Good news.

Beehive - Prosperity.

Beetle - Scandal.

Bell - Unexpected news.

Bellows - Setbacks.

Bird - Good news.

Birdcage - Obstacles, quarrels.

Bird's nest - Domestic harmony.

Bishop - Good luck coming.

Boat - Visit from a friend.

Book Open - Expect legal actions, future success.

Boomerang - Envy.

Boot - Achievement.

Bottle - Pleasure.

Bouquet - Love and happiness.

Bow - Scandal, gossip.

Box - Romantic troubles solved.

Bracelet - Marriage.

Branch With leaves - A birth.

Bread - Avoid waste.

Bridge - An opportunity for success.

Broom - Small worries disappear.

Buckle - Disappointments ahead.

Building - A move.

Bull - Quarrels.

Bush - New friends.

Butterfly - Frivolity.

Baby - Pregnancy, something new.

Ball - Completion.

Butterfly - Transition

C

Cab - Disappointment.

Cabbage - Jealousy.

Cage - A proposal.

Camel - Useful news.

Candle - Help from others.

Cannon - News from a soldier.

Cap - Trouble ahead – be careful.

Car - Good fortune.

Cart - Success in business.

Castle - Financial gain through marriage.

Cat - A quarrel.

Cattle - Prosperity.

Chain - An engagement or wedding.

Chair - An unexpected guest.

Cherries - A happy love affair.

Chessmen - Difficulties ahead.

Chimney - Hidden risks.

Church Ceremony - Unexpected money.

Cigar - New friends.

Circle - Success, a wedding.

Claw - A hidden enemy.

Clock - Avoid delay, think of the future.

Clouds - Trouble ahead.

Clover - Prosperity.

Coat - A parting, an end of a friendship.

Coffin - Bad news.

Coin - Repayment of debts.

Collar - Dependence on others for success and happiness.

Column - Promotion.

Comb - Deceit.

Comet - An unexpected visitor.

Compass - Travel, a change of job.

Corkscrew - Curiosity causing trouble.

Crab - An enemy.

Crescent - A journey.

Cross - Trouble, ill health.

Crown - Honour, success.

Cup - Reward for effort.

Curtain - A secret.

Cymbal - Insincere love.

China - Engagement.

Chair - A guest.

Clock - Better health.

Coin - Change in financial status.

D

Daffodil - Great happiness.

Dagger - Danger ahead, enemies.

Daisy - Happiness in love.

Dancer - Disappointment.

Deer - A dispute or quarrel.

Desk - Letter containing good news.

Devil - Evil influences.

Dish - Quarrel at home.

Dog - Good friends.

Donkey - Be patient.

Door - Strange occurrence.

Dot - Money.

Dove - Good fortune.

Dragon - Unforeseen changes, trouble.

Drum - Scandal, gossip, a new job, arguments.

Duck - Money coming in.

Dustpan - Strange news about a friend.

E

Eagle - A change for the better.

Ear - Unexpected news.

Earrings - Misunderstanding.

Easel - Artistic success.

Egg - Prosperity.

Eggcup - Danger is passing.

Elephant - Wisdom, strength.

Engine - News on its way fast.

Envelope - Good news.

Eye - Overcoming difficulties, take care.

F

Face - Setback.

Fairy - Joy and enchantment.

Fan - Flirtation.

Feather - Instability.

Feet - An important decision.

Fence - Limitation.

Fern - Disloyalty.

Fir - Artistic success.

Fire - Achievement.

Fireplace - Matters related to your home.

Fish - Good fortune in all things, health, wealth and happiness.

Fist - An argument.

Flag - Danger ahead.

Flower - Wish coming true.

Fly - Domestic irritations.

Font - A birth.

Fork - A false friend, flattery.

Forked Line - Decisions to be made.

Fountain - Future success and happiness.

Fox - A deceitful friend.

Frog - Success through a change of home or job.

Fruit - Prosperity.

G

Gallows - Social failure.

Garden roller - Difficulties ahead.

Garland - Success, great honour.

Gate - Opportunity, future happiness.

Geese - Invitations, unexpected visitors.

Giraffe - Think before you speak.

Glass - Integrity.

Glove - A challenge.

Goat - Enemies.

Gondola - Romance, travel.

Gramophone - Pleasure.

Grapes - Happiness.

Grasshopper - News from a friend.

Greyhound - Good fortune.

Guitar - Happiness in love.

Gun - Trouble, quarrels.

H

Hammer - Overcoming obstacles.

Hand - Friendship.

Handcuffs - Trouble ahead.

Hare - News of a friend.

Harp - Harmony in love.

Hat - A new occupation.

Hawk - Sudden danger, jealousy.

Head - New opportunities.

Heart - Love and marriage, a trustworthy friend.

Heather - Good fortune.

Hen - Domestic bliss.

Hill - Obstacles, setbacks.

Hoe - Hard work leading to success.

Holly - An important occurrence in the winter.

Horn - Abundance.

Horse Galloping - Good news from a lover.

Horseshoe - Good luck.

Hourglass - A decision that must be made.

House - Security.

I

Iceberg - Danger.

Initials - Usually those of people known to you.

Inkpot - A letter.

Insect - Minor problems soon overcome.

Ivy leaf - Reliable friend.

J

Jester - Party or social gathering.

Jewellery - A present.

Jug - Gaining in importance, good health.

K

Kangaroo - Domestic harmony.

Kettle - Minor illness.

Key - New opportunities.

Keyhole - Beware of idle curiosity.

King - A powerful ally.

Kite - Wishes coming true.

Knife - Broken relationships.

L

Ladder - Promotion.

Lamp - Money.

Leaf - Prosperity, good fortune.

Leopard - News of a journey.

Letter - News. Near dots - news about money.

Lighthouse - Trouble threatening.

Lines straight and clear - Progress, journeys.

Lines wavy - Uncertainty, disappointment.

Line slanting - Business failure.

Lion - Influential friends.

Lock - Obstacles in your path.

Loop - Impulsive actions could bring trouble.

M

Man - A visitor.

Map - Travel and change.

Mask - Deception.

Medal - A reward.

Mermaid - Temptation.

Monkey - A flattering mischief-maker.

Monster - Terror.

Monument - Lasting happiness.

Moon Full - A love affair.

Mountain - Obstacle, high ambition.

Mouse - Theft.

Mushroom - Growth, setbacks.

Music - Good fortune.

N

Nail - Malice.

Necklace complete - admirers.

Necklace broken - the end of a relationship.

Needle - Admiration.

Net - A Trap.

Numbers - Indicate a timescale, the number of days before an event occurs.

Nun - Quarantine.

Nurse - Illness.

Nutcrackers - Difficulty is passing.

O

Oak - Good fortune.

Oar - A small worry, help in difficulties.

Octopus - Danger.

Opera glasses - A quarrel, loss of a friend.

Ostrich - Travel.

Owl - Gossip.

Oyster - Courtship, acquired riches.

P

Padlock open - A surprise.

Padlock closed - A warning.

Palm tree - Success, honour, happiness in love.

Parachute - Escape from danger.

Parasol - A new lover.

Parcel - A surprise.

Parrot - A scandal, a journey.

Peacock - Riches.

Pear - Comfort.

Pentagon - Intellectual balance.

Pepper - A troublesome secret.

Pig - Material success.

Pigeon sitting - An improvement in trade.

Pigeon flying - Important news.

Pillar - Supportive friends.

Pipe - Thoughts, solution to a problem, keep an open mind.

Pistol - Danger.

Pitchfork - Quarrels.

Policeman - Secret enemy.

Pump - Generosity.

Purse - Profit.

Pyramid - Success.

Q

Question mark - Hesitancy, caution.

R

Rabbit - Timidity, be brave.

Railway - Long journey.

Rainbow - Happiness, prosperity.

Rake - Be organised.

Rat - Treachery.

Raven - Bad news.

Razor - Quarrels, partings.

Reptiles - Treacherous friend.

Rider - Hasty news.

Ring - Completion.

Rocks - Difficulties.

Rose - Popularity.

S

Saucepan - Anxieties.

Saw - Interfering outsider.

Scales - A lawsuit.

Sceptre - Power, authority.

Scissors - Domestic arguments, separation.

Scythe - Danger.

Shamrock - Good luck, wish coming true.

Sheep - Good fortune.

Shell - Good news.

Ship - Successful journey.

Shoe - A change for the better.

Sickle - Disappointment in love.

Signpost - Draws attention to the symbol to which it points.

Skeleton - Loss of money, ill health.

Snake - Hatred, an enemy.

Spade - Hard work leads to success.

Spider - Determined and persistent. Money coming.

Spoon - Generosity.

Square - A symbol of protection, comfort, peace.

Squirrel - Prosperity after a hard time.

Star - Good health, happiness.

Steeple - Slight delay, bad luck.

Steps - An improvement in life.

Sun - Happiness, success, power.

Swallow - Decisiveness, unexpected journeys.

Swan - Smooth progress, contented life.

Sword - Disappointment, quarrels.

T

Table - Social gathering.

Teapot - Committee meeting.

Telephone - Forgetfulness causes trouble.

Telescope - Adventure.

Tent - Travel.

Thimble - Domestic changes.

Toad - Beware of flattery.

Torch - A turn for the better.

Tortoise - Criticism.

Tower - Opportunity, Disappointment.

Tree - Changes for the better.

Triangle - Something unexpected.

Trunk - A long journey, fateful decisions.

U

Umbrella - Annoyances.

Unicorn - A secret wedding.

Urn - Wealth, happiness.

V

Vase - A friend in need.

Vegetables - Unhappiness followed by contentment.

Violin - Egotism.

Volcano - Emotions out of control.

Vulture - Loss, theft, an enemy in authority.

W

Wagon - A wedding.

Walking stick - A visitor.

Wasp - Trouble in love.

Waterfall - Prosperity.

Weather vane - A difficulty, indecisiveness.

Whale - Business success.

Wheel - Good fortune.

Wheelbarrow - A meeting with an old friend.

Windmill - Business success.

Window open - Good luck through a friend.

Window closed - disappointment through a friend.

Wings - Messages.

Wishbone - A wish granted.

Wolf - Jealousy, selfishness.

Woman - Pleasure.

Worms - Scandal.

Wreath - Happiness ahead.

Y

Yacht - Pleasure.

Yoke - Being dominated.

Z

Zebra – Overseas adventure.

Shapes

If you come across any of the following shapes in a reading you should pay particular attention to them:

TRIANGLES   Triangles equal good karma.

SQUARES   If you see a square there is need for caution.

CIRCLES   A circle equals great success in any venture.

LETTERS   Specific letters usually refer to names of friends and relatives.

NUMBERS   Indicates time, as in months and years.

Timing

You can predict when something is likely to happen by starting at the handle of the teacup. A teacup reading can only predict up to a year in the future. If you find tea-leaves stuck to the bottom of the cup, this will tell you that things will happen in about a year's time. Tea-leaves that are stuck near to the top of the cup indicate that events will happen within a few days or weeks.

Sometimes you will find clumps of tea-leaves stuck all over the cup from the bottom up towards the handle. This is quite common and is a sign of a lot of changes happening over the course of the next twelve months. To summarise this it is best to start at the bottom of the cup, and work backwards from twelve months. Look for any obvious symbols and their definitions and then work your way back up to the rim of the cup. This will give you an overall picture of what is forthcoming for the questioner.

For example; you may see the symbol of an urn and a wagon at the bottom of the cup and then further up the side you may see the symbol of a table and a heart. Towards the top you might see the shape of a bird. This would tell you that the questioner will soon find the love of her life, get married and be very happy with her life.

If you have trouble seeing any symbols in the cup, try closing your eyes and turning the cup in a clockwise direction again. What might have originally looked like a lump of tea-leaves may well resemble something different when you open your eyes again.

COFFEE READINGS

For those that prefer coffee, this is a modern alternative to reading tea-leaves. It is thought that the origins of coffee-cup readings stem from Arabia, who first discovered coffee beans around 600AD and kept it a secret for several hundred years. Coffee became known as a beverage in Western Europe in the late 18th century and coffee reading is as popular, if not more, today as tea-leaf reading with many coffee houses in America offering a Turkish coffee-reading service with your morning cuppa.

What you need to read coffee beans...

The ideal ground coffees to use in a coffee reading are African, Greek or Turkish beans, which are rich in taste as well as consistency. These can be found in most supermarkets or coffee shops. The drink should be brewed, ideally in a traditional long-handled briki. Do not add milk to the coffee. If the questioner is looking for the answer to a specific question, she should be thinking about this whilst sipping the coffee.

Reading the coffee beans...

Once the coffee is finished, drain any remaining liquid and then turn the cup clockwise three times. This will ensure that the sediment is evenly spread around the bottom of the cup.

Turn the cup over onto a napkin and leave it to rest for a few minutes. This is your time to ask for guidance in reading your cup or to concentrate on the question you wish to have answered.

Turn the cup upright again and look into it. How you interpret the symbols you see will be unique to you; what looks like a dog to you might look like something completely different to someone else. As with the symbols for tea-leaf readings, the same applies to coffee-cup readings.

Timing

As a general rule, the bottom of the cup represents people, ideas, situations or past events. The middle part up the side of the cup represents the present and the top part of the cup represents what is coming up in the future for you.

When you begin drinking your tea or coffee, make a note of the following:

- Bubbles on the surface of your tea or coffee show that money is coming to you.
- Tea-leaves that float on the surface of your tea reveal that visitors are on their way to you.
- If the teaspoon is placed upside down on the saucer of your cuppa when it is served to you, it is a sign of someone in your family being ill.

Some readers see specific letters within the cup and can be interpreted at such:

A The beginning of something.

B A fight.

E A big surprise.

F A new relationship.

G Pride

H Bravery.

I A surprise.

J Love.

K Use of something.

L Lies.

M Relief.

N Hope.

P Victory.

R Happiness.

T Punctuality.

X The unknown.

Z Protection.

When you have finished your reading, whether it is with the use of tea-leaves or coffee beans, it's customary to turn the cup over, place your index finger on the cup and make a wish.

Runes

Rune stones have been used as an oracle tool for thousands of years, originally deriving from the Vikings. According to tradition, the word Rune means 'a whispered secret.'

Today there are many different types of Rune stones made out of many different types of material. However, Rune stones were traditionally made out of pebbles so that they could be easily hidden among other pebbles, but couldn't be destroyed by fire. Pagans would use Runes to foretell what the future held for them between the winter sabbats of Samhain and Yule.

Many gypsies still use Rune stones today to give accurate readings. Depending on which system you use, there are usually 24 Runes in a set.

How to make your own set of Runes

Traditionally Rune stones would be made out of clay. The symbols would have been written on in the blood from a menstruating woman and then baked in a clay oven. I'm in no way suggesting you wait until your period to make your Rune stones – that would just be rather eww!

A far simpler way if you want to make your own personalised set of Rune stones is to either collect 24 similar sized pebbles, or, if you're feeling like a lumberjack, you can saw 24 segments from a thin branch of a tree, write one sign on each segment and varnish the wood, so that you have 24 individual disc shapes. You can of course go out and buy a set from any New Age store or online.

If you are considering making your own set of Runes, traditionally the symbols are written in red. Do this with a permanent marker, paint or red nail polish; anything that won't come off when the Runes are rubbing together in a bag.

If you are handy with a sewing machine, you can make a small pull-string bag to put your Runes in. Alternatively you can buy some very pretty Rune/Tarot bags specifically for this purpose.

The 24 Runes

Fehu

Wealth. Money. Prosperity.
The Fehu Rune is basically the sign of wealth and if you draw this stone, it means that money is on its way to you. In oldie-worldy times wealth would mean trading cattle for corn, rather than a top up in your bank account.

By picking this Rune, you can be assured that your finances are set to improve. This could be in the form of a new job bringing more money into your life, or it could be a lottery win, an unexpected inheritance or a second job, giving you a better income.

Uruz

Strength. Overcoming Obstacles.
Vikings would decorate their helmets with this sign in the belief that it would give them strength to help them in their battles.

Today, drawing this Rune stone is a way of telling you that whatever is going on in your life right now, you do have the strength to see if through. You may have had (or be going through) a challenging time lately, but if you can remain strong, you will pull through this difficult time. This also applies to other people. You may find that you have to be supportive to someone else and your strength will help them to get through any obstacles they face at the moment.

Thurisaz

Protection. Challenges. Secrets.

Thurisaz is the Rune of protection. Travelling gypsies would often carve this symbol into trees near to where they were staying to protect them and their belongings from intrusion, and you can still see this sign today in areas where gypsies have stayed.

It is associated with challenges and secrets. If someone is being deceptive to you, or not telling you the whole truth, this Rune is letting you know that you are protected from them and that the truth will soon be revealed.

Ansuz

Inspiration. Wisdom. Communication.

This is the sign of wisdom, new ideas and communication and originally told the tale of Odin, a mythological Norse god who was desperate to acquire the wisdom and knowledge of the older order of giants. He sacrificed one of his eyes in exchange for wisdom and was highly regarded as the chap to turn to if you needed information – a bit like Google.

By drawing this Rune you are being told that information is on the way which will inspire you to become more knowledgeable. If you're thinking of re-training or studying in some way, then this is giving you the green light to go for it. Communication is also highlighted here, so if you've been waiting for someone to contact you, then you won't have much longer to wait.

Raidho

Journeys. Travel. Change.
Raidho is the Rune associated with travel and change. When you draw this Rune it suggests that you are about to embark on a journey – this could be a physical journey such as going on holiday, re-locating for work or moving home. It can also mean an emotional journey. A journey always has a beginning and an end, so if it's more of an emotional journey, you will be nearing the end of any difficulties soon and will be able to look back and see that you have been on some sort of life-changing challenge.

Kenaz

Guidance. Inner strength.
Kenaz is the Rune associated with guidance and strength. If you've been having a difficult time of late, picking this Rune is telling you not to worry and that things will be alright very soon. Often we need to go through difficult times in order to learn a lesson, or understand more about ourselves and others. Probably not what you want to hear right now, but there really is light at the end of the tunnel. Everything in life does happen for a reason.

Gebo

A Gift.
This is a lovely Rune to pick in a reading because it signifies a gift of some sort coming to you. This could be in the form of an actual gift such as a present, or it could be an exchange of something, like the love of someone new or even a marriage proposal. This is also a reminder that you already have a wonderful gift – the gift of life. Too often we take this for granted, especially if things haven't been going to plan.

Winjo

Joy. Happiness. Success.
This Rune represents happiness through your own efforts, so if you've been struggling to get the recognition you deserve, then it will soon come. By picking this Rune everything is about to fall into place and you will be not only singing, but dancing for joy! Whatever you are hoping will come about, this Rune is telling you that it is all about to happen.

Hagalaz

Disruption.
This particular Rune is known as the Mother Rune and is one that

foretells disruption in your life. This could be in the form of outside influences, or in the way that you think and judge others. Whilst disruption is always a bit daunting at first – no one likes forced change, after all – often the reluctance to change can mean we stay stuck as we are, whilst others move on. Accept that change is inevitable and that we need change in order to grow.

Naudhiz

Needs.
This Rune is all about our needs and how we go about getting those needs met. It is our needs that drive us to achieve things, whether this is the need for money, love or something else. We all have needs and desires. This Rune suggests that your needs will be met, but you will have to put in the hours or work required to get what it is you want.

Isa

Freeze. Hibernate.
Drawing the Isa Rune it's a way of telling you to stop for five minutes and just be for a while. Just as nature stands still during the winter season, so too are you being advised to pull back for a bit and not rush into anything right now. As with the nature analogy, while it looks as though nature has stopped, things are happening below the surface. You might not think they are, but they are. Have a bit of patience and things you want to happen will do.

Jera

Harvest. Results.
Jera represents the harvest of something. In the good ole' days, this would have been a good sign for farmers who feared their crops would never come to fruition. Today it's more to do with getting the results you want from the hard work you've put in. This could be exams, job hunting, sticking through the tough times in a relationship or jumping over obstacles that have been put in your way. There's an old saying; you reap what you sow. This means that although times might have been tough, you will soon see it was worth all the effort.

Eihwaz

Endings and beginnings.
This Rune often shows up when something is coming to an end. In the Tarot you would draw the Death card. I can't emphasise enough that we need change in our life in order for us to grow. This could be the end of a relationship that is doing you no good, the end of a job you hate, or the end of a friendship that has been more of a pain than a pleasure. Remember, although change is a bit scary, often it's because we are habitual creatures and like things to stay the same. When you look back on this time you will see that the change was needed so that new and exciting things could come into your life.

Perthro

Chance. Gamble.
Perthro is known as the 'Rune of Destiny'. Often we overanalyse what's happening in our lives to the extent that we end up going round in circles. Sometimes it's necessary to take a gamble and let fate decide what's best for you. In Norse times, they would make decisions based on the will of the gods. This Rune is telling you to take a chance. If you continue to do what you've always done, you will continue to get what you've always got. Do something different now and see what happens. Not everything has to be planned or mapped out.

Elhaz

Spiritual Growth.
You wouldn't be reading this book if you didn't have an interest in spiritual things and this Rune is telling you to explore different areas of interest because you may just find the answers you're looking for. We live in a world now where everything is just a click away, so use this to your advantage to explore different spiritual areas. As clever as we are, we don't know all the answers to those why-are-we-here questions, but by drawing this Rune, it's telling you to go and find out and you might be pleasantly surprised by the outcome.

Sowilo

Victory. Success. Joy.

This is a lovely Rune to pick because it is telling you that you are about to have a fabulous time! The sun was precious to the Norse gods and it's surrounded in mythology – many people still celebrate the Summer Solstice today, because without it earth wouldn't exist. This Rune is a sign that things are about to take a very positive turn for you. This could be in your love life, career, college or any other area. If you've been struggling with something, this is a sign that you will win. Success is just on the horizon.

Tiwaz

Guiding star. Have faith.

Tiwaz was a Norse god who looked after all matters of justice. By picking this Rune you are being told to have faith because all will come right in the end. If you've been the subject of bullying, victimisation, discrimination or feel that you have been treated unfairly, this is a sign to tell you that the perpetrators will get what's coming to them. It's a form of Karma; if people go around treating people badly, it will come back bite them on the bum! Have faith that someone 'up there' is looking out for you and it will all be OK.

Berkano

Renewal.
Berkano is the Rune relating to Mother Earth and is telling you it's time to start thinking about yourself for once, instead of thinking about others' needs all the time. We all have a habit of trying to cram as much as we can into 24 hours. I don't mean to sound like your mother, but partying every night of the week is all very well, but it will take its toll on your health. Our bodies need time to regenerate themselves and they can't do this if we don't allow ourselves time to rest. Boring, I know, but essential if you're to be happy and healthy!

Ehwaz

Loyalty. Moving on. Friendship.
Ehwaz is associated with the horse, which was an animal sacred to the Vikings because of the help that a horse gave to warriors riding into battle. By picking this Rune you are being reassured that you have lots of friends and help around you right now – and I'm not talking those 'friends' on Facebook. There could be a house move on the cards or new people coming into your life very soon and they will be very loyal to you. Alternatively, if you've been attracting far too many frogs recently, then this is a sign that your prince is riding his way into your life – probably not on a horse, but you never know.

Mannaz

Human Nature. Weakness. Strength.
When you pick this Rune it's a sign of a gathering or a group of people with one thing in common. This could be a sign that you will join a new club, meet lots of different people at a party, or start something new where there will be lots of people. There's also a message in this Rune that reminds us that we are all human. When someone is off with you for no apparent reason, try to remember that they are human too and they have exactly the same hang ups as you do. They worry about the same things as you, and they have bad days too.

Laguz

Birth. New beginnings. Emotions.
Laguz is the Rune of beginnings. Whilst this often appears when someone is pregnant, it's also a sign that new beginnings are on the way for you. This could be a new relationship, a new job offer, or a completely new way of life. Regardless, the message is, it is always positive news.

Ingwaz

Creation. Home. Protection.
Ingwaz is another fertility Rune, but it also represents the home

and home life. Ingwaz was an old Germanic earth god who looked after the home and the family. This Rune is telling you to find comfort in your home and family right now. Family are there no matter what and although certain members can be a pain from time to time, they will always be on your side and there to protect you. We often take our families for granted. This Rune is telling you to give them a break and enjoy each other's company. Funny enough, this stone often shows up before a family celebration or Christmas.

Othala

Home. Domestic matters. Finances.
Othala is another Rune that is all to do with your home life and your family. It's also a reminder that we are all responsible for helping other people who live with us. If we don't, then resentment sets in and that's when you get family arguments. It's important to remember that looking after a family doesn't come with a handbook and that your parents, or whoever you are living with, are only doing their best. We are all learning on a day-to-day basis. This is also a sign that your finances are about to improve. This could be connected to your family or their support.

Dagaz

Awakening. Light at end of the tunnel.
This Rune represents the Norse legend that day will follow night

and vice-versa. Nott, the goddess of night, was also the creator of light. She had a son with Dellinger (meaning dawn), who was known as Dag (meaning day). This is a sign that things are going to get better. Just as night follows day, there is light at the end of the tunnel and nothing stays the same. Yesterday is now history, so don't waste your energy dwelling on what's happened or what might have been. Look forward to a new day and enjoy it.

How to do a Rune reading

Once you have all your Runes, place them in a cloth bag and give the bag a little shake. Think of a question you want answered or an answer to a situation. Put your hand into the bag of Runes and swish them around a bit. Pick three Rune stones out. These will represent your past, present and future in answer to your question. Read the meanings of the Runes for an overall answer.

If you want a more in-depth reading, pick a further three Runes from the bag. These stones should throw more light on to the answer.

As with all the techniques in this book, you can make up your own readings. So, for example, you might want to use the same amount of Runes as is in your name, or you might want to draw four stones to represent the month ahead. All divination systems tap into your subconscious which already knows all the answers. Play around with different types of readings and you will soon see how accurate they are.

Dominoes and Dice

Divination by Domino

If you're looking for a very simple and easy way of predicting your fortune and have a set of dominoes to hand then there is no better way to get fast and accurate answers to your questions.

It has been claimed that English gypsies originally told fortunes using dominoes rather than Tarot or playing cards because they were easier to hide. Today, many gypsies still follow this tradition to gain insight into their futures. As with Tarot/card readings, there are many different spreads, but for a simple past, present and future reading see below:

You will need

A full set of dominoes.
A bag in which to keep them safe.
Tradition says that you should never read the dominoes on a Monday or a Friday.

Place the set of dominoes in the bag and concentrate on the question or situation you wish to be answered. The first domino you draw relates to your past, the second your present and the third, your future. The meanings of the dominoes are as below:

Blank

The blank domino usually refers to trouble ahead. If it can go wrong, it probably will. Plans will be delayed, arguments will surface and disagreements will ensure. However, drawing the blank domino doesn't mean you're set for a life of doom and gloom. It is a warning which will prepare you to be on your guard.

0 – 1

Drawing a blank and the number one warns that an old enemy is about and forewarns you to watch out for someone who might suddenly come back into your life. They might be all sweetness and light to start with, but watch out because this person is not what he/she first seems.

0 – 2

Drawing a blank with the number two is telling you to watch what you spend at the moment. You may think you have more in the bank than you actually do, or an unexpected bill might land on the doorstep, so keep a little back just in case.

0 – 3

The blank and a three tells of trouble in love. Someone you care deeply about could be deceiving you or not telling you the whole truth, so it's time to sit them down and have a heart to heart with them.

0 – 4

Drawing a blank and a four domino signals that there could be some money problems ahead of you. Double check contracts before signing anything and make sure that you don't leave your purse or handbag lying around unattended anywhere. Now would be a good time to go through your finances.

0 – 5

Is your marriage in trouble? It could be if you draw a domino with a blank and a five on it. Make some time to talk to your partner if you feel that things are not what they once were. If you're not married this domino tells of a lack of communication between two people.

0 – 6

Drawing a blank and the number six tells you that someone is talking about you. You may discover that someone you once thought was your friend is far from it and is only pretending to be your friend in order to get information out of you.

1 – 1

This lovely domino tells of a happy reunion ahead. Someone you haven't seen for ages is about to pop up in your life and you will look back on happy memories together. This also signals a happy time for friendship, so get on the phone and get in touch with old friends.

1 – 2

This domino signals that you will soon receive a visit from an old friend. You may not have seen each other for some time, but that won't be a problem when you get together again because it will be just like old times.

1 – 3

The domino with a one and a three signifies success in business or a successful trip ahead of you. If you're thinking of starting a business or looking for a new job then this domino is giving you the green light to go ahead and do it. You can't fail!

1 – 4

The domino with a one and a four is warning you to watch your pennies right now and don't take on any new debts at the moment. If you have your heart set on something, ask yourself if you are prepared to wait and save up for it. Getting into debt is easy, getting out of debt is harder.

1 – 5

The one and five domino signals the start of a love affair! Watch out for someone who tries to catch your eye at a party or other social event. Cupid is firing his arrow in your direction right now and you will soon be very lucky in love!

1 – 6

The one and six domino tells of a very happy marriage ahead for you, so if you are about to get married, then this is telling you that he is The One and that you will be very happy. If you are not currently in a relationship, you soon will be.

2 -2

The wishing domino! The two twos signal a wish comes true for you very soon. Whatever you want can be yours if you remain positive and believe that it is yours. Think about what you desire the most and then make a wish – it will come true.

2 – 3

Expect an unexpected windfall soon. The two and three domino tells of money coming in, so you can splash out a bit and buy yourself something nice. Now is the time to buy an extra lottery ticket or enter a competition because you might just win.

2 – 4

The two and four domino signifies deception or theft, so be on the lookout for someone trying to pull the wool over your eyes. Check references of people offering to do work for you and make sure you keep an eye on your purse and handbag.

2 – 5

The two and five domino is telling you to watch out for someone who is out to cause trouble. This could be a friend or someone you barely know. Keep your opinions to yourself at the moment because someone will try to twist your words and make you out to be the bad guy.

2 – 6

Drawing the two and six domino tells that you will have good luck in business. If you are thinking of starting a business or are already in business for yourself then Lady Luck is shining on you now. Network as much as possible because this will give you the opportunity to make new contacts.

3 – 3

The double three domino is a sign that a windfall on its way to you. This could be in the form of a financial win, an unexpected inheritance or winning a competition. Take chances now. You will find that it will be in your favour if you do.

3 – 4

This domino shows that you will be happy in love. If you are in a relationship then it can only get better. If you are single then look out because someone is about to fall head over heels in love with you. Your love life is blossoming now – you lucky thing!

3 – 5

The three and five domino tells that you will soon have visitors from abroad. An unexpected phone call, letter or email with an announcement will confirm details and you will soon be making up the guest bed. Expect a time of fun catching up with an old friend.

3 – 6

The three and six domino signals an unexpected gift coming to you. Keep an eye out for the postman because this is a time for surprises coming your way. If you are thinking of signing a contract then this is the time to do it.

4 – 4

A double four domino signals that a party or celebration is ahead for you, so get your best party frock and dancing shoes out and wait for the invitations to arrive. A double four can also signal a birth announcement.

4 – 5

The four and five domino is telling you that a happy surprise is ahead for you. Pay rises, unexpected presents or gifts or just some happy news are all highlighted now and you will be feeling very happy and fulfilled.

4 – 6

This domino signifies a happy marriage with children. If you are married then you can expect it to be a very happy one surrounded by happy children. If you are free and single then you won't be for long. Expect to find your soul mate very soon.

5 – 5

A change in fortune.

5 – 6

A new house.

6 – 6

Happiness ahead, say goodbye to any worries.

If you want to find out what the coming year has in store for you, pick a domino and add up the total amount of dots on it.

1. Misfortune.
2. Meeting someone new.
3. Expect the unexpected.
4. A new job where you will be the leader.
5. Domestic problems ahead.
6. Double check when thinking of investing your money.

7. A visitor will have a big impact on you.
8. Don't take the blame for someone else's mistakes.
9. A change in fortune for the better.
10. You will reach your goals this year.
11. A new friendship.
12. A new hobby gives you hope and love.

Did You Know?

Dominoes are thought to have come from China.

Dominoes were originally made out of wood.

More than $750,000 dollars can be won in the annual World Championship Domino Tournament.

DIVINATION BY DICE

It's not clear where the divination by dice came from, but it almost certainly derived as a Victorian parlour game during the late 1800s. Divination by dice is a very simple way of predicting your near future and answering questions you may have.

What you need

Three dice

A cup to shake the dice in (optional)

A large piece of white card

Scissors

A compass (like the one you used in school)

Or a plate, 7 inches in diameter

A pen

Draw a circle that is 7 inches in diameter on your piece of card and cut it out with the scissors. This will be your casting circle.

Think of a question you wish to be answered and place the dice in the cup. Gently blow into the cup and shake the cup (keep one hand on top to stop them from spilling out). Alternatively you can cup your hands.

Throw the three dice into the casting circle. Add up the numbers of the upper surface of the dice. Folklore says that you shouldn't cast the dice more than three times in any one day and that you shouldn't cast the dice on a Monday, because this will bring bad luck.

Total Interpretation

3 Sudden changes, but good ones.
4 Expect arguments or disagreements.
5 What you now desire will happen. A wish come true.
6 A possible financial loss.
7 You may be presented with a difficult matter/problem to solve.
8 Not everyone will support you.
9 A marriage or new partnership ahead.
10 Birth of a baby or a new project.
11 A parting with someone, but only temporary.
12 An important message in the form of a letter, text or email.
13 Sorrow and loss, followed by success.
14 Help from a good friend or family member.
15 Wait before committing yourself to something.
16 A good journey, holiday or trip.
17 A quick change of plans is ahead for you.
18 The luckiest number! Good fortune and luck is on the way.

If any dice roll outside of the circle or fall to the floor before reaching the circle, the following interpretations can be used.

1 **di outside the circle** Difficulties or an upset
2 **dice outside the circle** Arguments or disagreements
3 **dice outside the circle** Luck or a wish to come true

Any dice on the floor Problems, worry or annoyance very soon

Suggestions to ask the dice

You can ask the dice any question for a quick answer. Below are some suggestions.

Relationships

Is the one I'm with, really The One?
Should we move in together?
Which one should I choose to be with?

Career

Should I stay in the job I hate?
Will I get another job soon?
Should I set up my own business?

Health/wellbeing

Will this diet work?
When will I be happy?
Should I join the gym?

Wealth

Will I get rich soon?
Should I get a second job?
Should I take a financial gamble?

Divination with dice is the same as any divination system. It is a tool to tap into your subconscious mind, which already knows the answers. Obviously the answers are not entirely specific to your specific question, so think about what the answer means in relation to your question.

Ribbon Readings

Ribbons are not just useful items for tying your hair up or adding the finishing touches to a present, they can also act as a great tool for an insight in to your future...

Ribbons used in readings date back to Celtic times and folklore tales of travelling gypsies, offering their handmade crafts and bright-coloured ribbons, reveal that when they sold a ribbon, usually for ladies to wear in their hair or to attach to their clothes, they would also give them a free ribbon reading, depending on the colour ribbon they bought.

How to do your own Ribbon Readings...
Ribbon Readings are a good way to not only predict the outcome of your future, but also give you a good idea of who you really are. As with any form of divination, for a Ribbon Reading to be successful, it is essential to find a place where you can have five minutes' peace and quiet. Prior to using your ribbons, leave them laid out on a window-sill that catches the light of a full moon. This will cleanse and energise each individual ribbon.

What you will need
14 plain-coloured ribbons (about 12 inches in length).

The colours should be: Light pink, dark pink, orange, green, peach, turquoise, navy blue, light blue, purple, silver, white, red, black, yellow.

Three patterned ribbons (about 12 inches in length).

A silk or velvet purse or a small wooden box to keep the ribbons in.

How to read your ribbons
Place all the ribbons inside your silk purse or wooden box and give them a little mix around. Now you can begin your reading.

Think of a question or a situation you want answered or resolved, and without looking in the bag/box take out one ribbon and place it on a table in front of you. Repeat this six more times – be sure to remember the order of the ribbons you have taken out. You may find it's easier to lay them so that the first is the top, the second below it and so on. Starting from the top, your ribbons relate to the following areas of your life:

Ribbon One: Your personality and who you are.
Ribbon Two: Any negative aspects in relation to your question/situation.
Ribbon Three: Any positive aspects in relation to your question/situation.
Ribbon Four: Suggested action to take.
Ribbon Five: Your strengths.
Ribbon Six: Your weaknesses.
Ribbon Seven: The outcome.

Read each ribbon in order. Below is a list detailing the meaning of each ribbon:

Red – You are passionate and fiery, but may find it difficult to maintain a steady relationship. Red ribbons also show someone who needs to become more spiritual in order to be happy. Remember, material things are not the be all and end all. Home and family are important to you. A marriage proposal could be on the way.

Black – Black is the sign of protection. You are very protective of yourself and family. Black can signal that you have been through an emotional time lately. This colour is also associated with someone who is drawn to all things of an occult nature, so you would be advised to listen to your intuition. Watch out for someone who is not all they seem.

Light Pink – You are open and tend to wear your heart on your sleeve, however you are very positive and optimistic in life. Don't take everything so personally and try not to take on other people's emotions.

Dark Pink – As above, but you are much more open with your feelings and emotions, which is not always a good thing. Try to hold back a little and don't reveal everything about yourself too soon.

Orange – You tend to take things to excess and have a bit of an addictive personality. The advice here is to try and calm down a bit. If an offer looks too good to be true, it probably is. Listen to your inner voice, it's always right.

Peach – Be your own best friend. You can be your own worst enemy sometimes. Don't let other people influence you too much. Decisions might have to be made, so weigh up the pros and cons before coming to a decision.

Yellow – You have good prospects if you choose the yellow ribbon and will get to where you want to easily. Money, success and prosperity are close by and this happy, sunny ribbon tells that life is good.

Green – Passionate and loving about nature, this ribbon suggests that you are happier in the great outdoors. Don't give too much to others. The message here is to find a balance between giving and receiving.

Turquoise – This shows that you are a strong character and often act as a support to others. You recover quickly from illness and can take huge amounts of stress. You are a natural advisor, but be careful that someone doesn't take it for granted.

Navy Blue – Blues are associated with having a natural talent for mediumship, clairvoyance and all things of a supernatural nature. Your talents in this area will soon grow and you should go with your gut instinct.

Light Blue – As with navy blue, but you are not yet aware of your talents. Find a spiritual circle or support where you can grow your talents and mix with like-minded people.

Purple – You are a natural carer and nurturer and have a real zest for life. Use this to your advantage. People are drawn to you like a magnet and you often play the role of the nurturer.

Silver – You are a young head on old shoulders. Wise beyond your years you would be wise to investigate past life regression. Looking back on your family tree will reveal many interesting secrets.

White – Like the simplicity of the colour white, you like a simple life. Get rid of anything that is holding you back. Clear out the old clutter in your life, so that you can live in harmony.

Patterned Ribbons
If you choose a patterned ribbon, first look carefully at the colours within the patterns and read the relevant colours. If the pattern is:

Stripy – This ribbon shows that you can be a bit prickly at times, but you are also a born organiser. Use this skill to get to the top of the ladder. You don't have the best patience with people sometimes, so try to learn a little.

Spotty – This shows that you are well balanced, but a little disorganised. You can be prone to overspending. Try to curb the overindulging too.

Zigzags – This shows that you have the ability to get on with people from all walks of life. Use this to your advantage. You would make a good counsellor, mentor or Samaritan.

A Sample Reading

Rebecca wanted to know what the future held for her and her boyfriend of two years, Tom. She chose the following ribbons:

Yellow, Black, light pink, white zigzags, green, red, white.

The first ribbon represents Rebecca's personality and shows that she is a happy-go-lucky-girl by nature, she is easy-going and nothing really phases her.

The second ribbon shows that she is very protective of Tom and that this is not always a good thing. It can sometimes push another person away.

The third ribbon highlights that Tom is happy with Rebecca's personality. Her optimism for life is what he loves about her.

The fourth ribbon suggests that Rebecca tends to overthink about her relationship and is advised to chill a bit.

The fifth ribbon shows that Rebecca's strengths are in giving and loving.

The sixth ribbon highlights that Rebecca often gets emotional and overanalyses the situation when there really is no need.

The seventh and final ribbon shows that if Rebecca can learn to relax a bit more and stop worrying about her relationship with Tom, it will flourish.

Pendulum Readings

From its discovery in 1602, the pendulum was originally used to tell the time. However, gypsies from all over the world have used the pendulum as a form of divination to tap into your intuition to answer any question you might have. Before the advent of sonograms, it was common for pregnant women to consult a pendulum reader to tell her the sex of her unborn child and this is still practiced today in many gypsy families, as is the practice of finding out the sex of the baby. In fact, a friend of mine used this technique to predict that I would have three daughters.

Professional pendulum readers can suspend a pendulum over a map and give accurate details of missing or lost objects – ideal for those times you put your phone down and can't remember where you put it! Pendulum divination has also been used for remote dowsing and has even been known to track down missing persons by using a pendulum over a map.

What you need

You can buy pendulums quite cheaply from New Age stores, or you can make one yourself, or even use a necklace chain and pendant.

To make your own

You need a length of ribbon about 12 inches in length.
Tie a small gemstone or pendant to the bottom of the ribbon.
Simples!

How to use your pendulum

When you first use your pendulum, you need to find out which way it swings for the answer 'yes' and which way it swings for the answer 'no'.

To do this, sit quietly at a table that will support your elbow comfortably. Hold the top of your pendulum between your index finger and your thumb and rest your elbow on the table. Use your other hand to stop the pendulum from swinging, so that it hangs in a straight line.

Close your eyes and ask the following question out loud:

Is the sun hot?

Wait a few moments and open your eyes. Keep repeating the question and watch to see which way the pendulum swings. It might swing round in a clockwise/anticlockwise direction, or it might swing back and forth in a straight line. Make of note of this because this is the answer *'yes'* to your question.

Next, straighten the pendulum again, close your eyes and ask the following question out loud:

Is a ball square?

Again, observe which way the pendulum swings. It should swing in a different way for the answer *'no'*. This can take some practice and it's easy to let your conscious mind take over resulting in you actually moving the pendulum, but keep practicing until you are sure it's the pendulum and not your conscious mind moving it.

Once you are sure you know the signs for your answers, you can begin to do your pendulum readings.

It's better if you can ask questions that require a yes or no answer. Sometimes if the pendulum has no answer it will swing for both answers. This is a sign to leave that particular question for another day and try again with another question.

Below are some suggestions for questions you can ask:

Is he/she The One?
Should I go out with (name)?
Should I go to the party?
Should I go back to college?
Is this the right course for me to take?
Will I get engaged?

Will I get married?
Will I move house soon?
Will I get that job?
Will I pass my exam?
Will I pass my driving test?
Will I have children?
Should I start my own business?
Should I finish my relationship?
Is he/she cheating on me?

Obviously, you can make up your own questions, so long as they are *'yes'* or *'no'* type questions.

The more you use your pendulum, the more experienced you get, the more detailed readings you will be able to do.

If you want to know whether you will have children, take a silver chain with one of your own rings attached to it to act as the pendulum. Hold the pendulum over your right palm and ask it questions using the yes and no technique. First ask whether you will have children. Secondly, ask will you have one, two, three, or more. Finally ask if you will have a girl, then if you will have a boy. You will be given the answers as a yes or a no.

If you are already pregnant, or know someone who is, a traditional Romany technique for working out whether the baby will be a boy or a girl is to thread the mum-to-be's wedding ring through a cord or ribbon and suspend it over her belly. If the ring moves in a distinct circle, the baby will be a girl. If the ring moves up and down or back and forth in a straight line, it will be a boy.

All Things Angels

We've all heard of angels and you may have even called upon them from time to time. Angels have been featured heavily (or even heavenly) in every culture for thousands of years. The nice thing about angels is that there is no stigma to believing in them. Unlike some supernatural/paranormal subjects, it's actually pretty cool and accepted to believe in angels. They are featured highly in films, books and TV series and you only have to look in any high-street store and you will see angels on t-shirts, notebooks, key chains, DVDs. They're everywhere and most people will happily talk about their experiences of angels, or will debate whether or not angels exist.

I'm a firm believer in angels and call on them to help me out with the big and little things that life throws at me from time to time. Whether it's finding a space in the car park, or saving my baby daughter from being crushed to death by a lorry (you can read my story in the *Chicken Soup for the Soul* book, *Angels Among Us*), I'm 100% sure that angels are there, if only you ask for their help.

Sometimes life doesn't always go quite according to plan and this is where angels can come into play. You don't have to be a firm believer in God, or any other religion, come to that, to believe in angels. We all have a guardian angel from birth, who looks after us throughout our lives. You don't have to know their name, you can just literally ask your guardian angel to help you, as and when you need it.

There is some debate among people that are self-imposed spiritualists who say that you should only call upon the angels in a matter of life and death. I disagree. There are no rules to say when you can call on an angel, or how many times you can ask them for help, or for what. If you need something minor such as a car parking space, ask. Angels are there to make our lives easier. Sometimes life may throw us a bum deal: you may be dreading going to school, college or work, or you may have too much month left over and not enough money to pay your rent, or you could be having a really bad time with your family, or be in a crappy relationship and need some guidance. Whatever the problem, however big or small, you can always call on the angels to help you.

Archangels

Whilst we all have our own guardian angels, there are five main higher archangels; **Michael, Raphael, Gabriel, Chamuel** and **Uriel** who you have probably heard of through books, films or the odd religious studies lesson. Anyone can call on these higher angels at any time and they are there to help you whatever your problem. There are a number of other archangels, but these five are the most powerful to call upon. All archangels are considered to be good angels and folklore has it that Satan, otherwise known as Lucifer, was once such an angel, until he fell from God's grace.

By calling upon an archangel for help your prayers will soon be answered, but these archangels have different skills for different needs, as follows:

Archangel Raphael

Archangel Raphael is the archangel in charge of healers and healing for all of earth's population. Raphael is the one to call on whenever you need some healing, whether it's physical or emotional. He is someone who will inspire you with ideas and will guide you back to feeling 100% yourself again.

When asked for healing assistance, Raphael surrounds and nurtures people with the emerald green light of his halo. Green is the colour of healing and people have often commented that they have seen emerald green sparkles when Raphael is around. Raphael also helps with relationship problems, grief and stressful family relations, so if you've been having a rough time of it emotionally, simply say his name and ask him to come to your side and help, saying something along the lines of, "Archangel Raphael, please come to my side and help me feel better about [issue]. Please surround me in your healing energy and guide my actions and thoughts so that I am healed."

Raphael is the archangel in charge of travel. As you check in at the airport, ask Raphael to watch over your luggage, the plane and your passport. Raphael and the traveller angels can give you directions when you're lost, keep a deflated tyre inflated, prevent your car from running out of petrol and even find you a parking space. He really is the ideal stress reliever. Don't forget to thank Archangel Raphael for his help.

Healing Meditation with Archangel Raphael

You can work with Archangel Raphael and his healing energy using this meditation.

Sit comfortably where you will not be disturbed. Close your eyes and imagine roots growing from your feet into the earth. Breathe in through your nose, hold it for seven seconds, and release it very slowly through your mouth. Repeat three times then continue breathing this way throughout the meditation. Call Archangel Raphael, either mentally or out loud and ask. *"Archangel Raphael, please come to me now and assist me in my healing."*

Picture Raphael standing over you with his hands outstretched over your head. See the healing energy in the form of green light flowing from his hands down into your body through the top of your head. If you don't feel anything at first, don't worry, just relax. It will come to you. Many people feel the healing energy as warmth or tingling.

Focus onto specific parts of your body that you want to be healed. If you are experiencing stress or emotional problems, imagine Raphael gently massaging your head. When you feel relaxed enough, open your eyes.

Archangel Michael

Archangel Michael is also known as Beshter, Mikail and Sabbathiel and is said to be the first archangel created by God. He is the leader of strength, protection, integrity and truth and helps us with our life purpose. When things seem to be going all the wrong way, Michael is there to help bring back some balance and focus in your life and calm you down a little.

Michael helps us to get back to basics and start over. He is the one to call upon if a relationship is getting too much to handle or if you find that you're experiencing the same health problems over and over again.

He will boost your immune system and help you to cope with challenging emotional difficulties and guide you to less stressful situations and opportunities. You will know when Michael is about because you can usually hear his voice. He is one of the few angels who actually speak to you and won't mince his words. Many also report that when they have spoken to Archangel Michael they feel as if they have learned a lesson. If you have a demanding job with tight deadlines, then this is the guy you need to turn to. He will leave you with a feeling of peace and hope and make you acknowledge that it's really not the end of the world and that all things come to pass and that this will too.

A Prayer to Archangel Michael

St. Michael the Archangel,
defend me from battle;
Be my safeguard
against the malice and snares
of the negative seen or unseen energy forces.
Rebuke the negative energy forces, oh God
I humbly beseech you,
and do thou oh prince of the heavenly host,
by the Divine Power of God
thrust into the darkness,

all the negative seen and unseen energy forces,
and all of the ugly spirits who wander about the world
seeking the ruination of souls.
In Jesus Christ's name I pray,
who lives and reigns with the Father and the Holy Spirit
One God
forever and ever.
Amen

Archangel Gabriel

The Archangel Gabriel is the archangel depicted as female in art and literature, and she is widely known as the "messenger" angel. Her name can be found in many different religions and is considered to be one of the two highest-ranking angels in Judeo-Christian and Islamic religious lore. Apart from Michael, she is the only angel mentioned by name in the Old Testament. She is a powerful and strong archangel, and if you call upon her, you will find yourself pushed into action, resulting in positive outcomes.

Gabriel was the angel who brought the message to Mary about the birth of Jesus, so if you are thinking of starting a family, she is the one to call on to help you. Gabriel often appears in dreams and visions and is the best communicator you could choose to have on your side. She is also a dab hand at kicking your butt into gear if you are fond of procrastination!

Gabriel also helps us to find our true purpose, so if you feel you have lost your way, call out to her and she will be able to get you back on track. If you are thinking about moving house, or making major life changes, Gabriel is the one to turn to, to ensure everything runs smoothly.

Gabriel is also the one to turn to if your health is a bit iffy right now. She will clear out any toxins in your body and change your attitude from negative to positive. She's the best friend everyone should have and is only a call away.

An Angel Journal

You can do this with any of the archangels, but it works particularly well with Gabriel. Find the nicest hardback notebook that you can afford and treat yourself to a new pen – you could even go all out and buy a white feather pen. Whenever you have a problem, start a new fresh page in your notebook and write it down in as much detail as possible. Gabriel is your best friend, who you would tell anything to, so make sure your write down as much information as you can think of about the situation or problem you have.

Say out loud: 'Archangel Gabriel, I call upon you to help me with this problem today and thank you for your guidance in advance.'

Keep your journal somewhere safe. In a few days' time you may suddenly find a solution to your problem, or something will happen that will resolve the issue you are concerned about. Archangels work in mysterious ways, so keep an eye out for signs that are not completely obvious at the time, such as a chance encounter with a business owner when you've recently written down how much you hate your job!

Once your problem has been resolved, write down what happened. It's really easy to forget when magical things happen in our lives and this serves as a reminder that Gabriel really was listening.

Archangel Uriel

Archangel Uriel is said to be one of the wisest archangels because he offers practical solutions, knowledge and information, but in a very subtle and gentle way. You may not even realise he has answered your prayer until you suddenly come up with a brilliant new idea or solution to a problem, as if by magic.

It was Archangel Uriel who warned Noah of the impending flood, and he also showed people how to manifest things out of thin air. Derren Brown has nothing on Uriel! Added to this he is in charge of problem solving, spiritual understanding, studies, alchemy, weather, earth changes and writing. If you are the shy and retiring type, or often find yourself saying yes, when you really mean no, for fear of causing upset, then this is the guy for you. He reaffirms your place in the world and makes you realise that you are important in this world, just like everyone else on earth. He will give you reassurance and comfort when you feel as though you are always the underdog.

A Problem Shared

Whenever you feel as though life has thrown you a raw deal and that you seem to be at the beck and call of everyone around you, light a white candle – white being the purest and most spiritual colour – and write down all the things or people that are taking you for granted. Spend some time writing as many situations or problems down, from all the times your best friend has cancelled a night out in favour of her new boyfriend, to how you always seem to be the one who cleans up after everyone else while they sit on their bums enjoying life. Whatever gets your goat, write it down. Take a few moments to vent your rage and really say what you feel. Don't worry, no one is going to read it but you. Take your piece of paper and the candle outside and say the following:

Uriel, I call upon you to help me out
May others learn to think about
My problems and let them see,
It's not all about them, sometimes it's about me!

Set the piece of paper alight and watch as the ashes fall to the ground. You should soon see that other people are less self-centred and more interested in your wellbeing than their own lives.

Archangel Chamuel

The Archangel Chamuel is the angel of pure love, and is one of the most loving angels you could ask for. Chamuel will lift you from the very depths of sadness and sort out everything concerning relationships, as well as helping you to find your soul mates in life. He is the angel who finds strong, lifelong relationships in all areas of your life and when you call upon him, you will feel butterflies in your tummy, because he works fast and efficiently.

If there's a breakdown in a relationship, whether it's work colleagues, family or romance, Chamuel will offer guidance and support to you. People who call upon Chamuel are very family orientated and try to solve all the problems in the world, but sometimes this can get wearing if you find you're constantly banging your head against a brick world. If you find your heart has become hardened and your mind is full of negative emotions, or you are depressed, call upon Chamuel to fix you. Chamuel is also a great locator of lost items, so if you are constantly losing your car keys, or those important memos on your desk, call on Chamuel to help you find them.

A Prayer to Help You Find True Love

When you feel that you just keep attracting no-goods, say this little prayer to help you find your soul mate.

Find a quiet place where you can sit undisturbed, switch off your phone and close your eyes for five minutes. Visualise Archangel Chamuel's golden light penetrating through the ceiling and casting you from head to toe in a warm orange light. Say the following words:

"In the name of God, I am all I am. In the name of Archangel Chamuel: Be gone forces of anti-love and replace this with pure love and light."

Repeat this nine times and then slowly open your eyes. You might feel a tingly feeling in your tummy. If you do this is a sure sign that Archangel Chamuel is listening to you.

A Few Angel Facts

All children have their own guardian angel.

Angels never die; they are immortal.

You do not have to believe in any specific god for angels to protect you.

Other Angels You Might Like

The recent double-dip recession has left most of us making cutbacks and tightening our belts and abundance of anything has been in short supply. But help is at hand. Angels are all around you at all times, but they won't interfere in your life unless your life is in danger. If you need abundance in your life, whether it is money, health or love, call on one of these angels to help you...

Angel:

Archangel Raziel

Call on this angel for:

Prosperity

Archangel Raziel is also known as the secret of God and is said to record all the information in the world. This angel knows everything about the universe and is there for when you find you have too much month left over and not enough money. He is the one to call on to bring you good fortune and financial wealth.

How to connect to this angel

Write down how much money you *need* (not how much money

you *want)* and be as specific as you can about what you need it for. Fold the paper into three and place it under your pillow. Say the following affirmation:

Archangel Raziel, I ask that you help to bring me the money I need and continue to send me prosperity from this day on.

Leave the note under your pillow until you receive the amount you have requested.

Angel:

Bakakiel

Call on this angel for:

Opportunity

Whether you are looking for a new job or a promotion, Barakiel, the ancient angel whose name means 'God's blessing' will assist you in your quest to bring opportunity to you. He often does so in the most mysterious and unusual ways. To connect with Barakiel, say the following prayer prior to going to an interview or a meeting with your boss.

'Barakiel, open my heart so that I may receive the blessings and opportunities that await me. It's here and it's now and I am inviting these gifts into my life. Help me stay positive and confident so that I can be a magnet of attraction, drawing everything into my life so I can experience my heart's desires.'

Angel:

Archangel Raphael

Call on this angel for:

Health

Archangel Raphael is the angel who looks after our health. He tunes into your body's vibrations and if they are out of line due to ill health, he will retune every part of your body so that you feel vibrant and full of beans again.

To call on Archangel Raphael, light a white tea-light candle and run a warm bath. Have no artificial lighting in the bathroom. Gaze into the flame and ask Raphael to send his healing to you. Close your eyes and feel the warmth from the candle radiating from the top of your head, all the way down through your body. Take as long as you feel necessary until you feel happy and better. It's best to do this last thing at night prior to going to bed.

Angel:

Gamaliel

Call on this angel for:

Gifts and Miracles

Gamaliel is one of the most generous angels to call upon when you are in need of money to buy gifts, such as expensive times like at Christmas or birthdays. He is known as the 'gracious gift giver' and is very powerful at creating the means to buy gifts for your loved ones. He likes nothing more than to please people, so call his name and he'll be there.

To call on Gamaliel, make a list of all the gifts you need to buy, fold the piece of paper into a square and tie with a small piece of ribbon, so that it looks like a small present. Leave this gift outside your front door. You should soon have enough money come to you to buy all the gifts in your life.

Angel:

Evelyn

Call on this angel for:

Manifesting

Evelyn is the angel of manifesting and is there for those times when we know what we want, but have no idea how to make it happen. Evelyn often comes to us in our dreams, giving us guidance or advice on how to manifest our hearts' desires. She will direct you to books, websites, people and other sources that will help you to manifest what you want.

To call on Evelyn, ask out aloud for what it is you want and then look out for signs that will be given to you. Evelyn works in a synchronistic way, so you will be drawn to the signs that will help you on your way. This could be in the form of an idea, a billboard you see on your way to work, or by bumping into someone who will help you. All you need to do is ask.

Did You Know?

The word *angel* comes from the Greek word *angellos*, which means messenger.

Angels do not marry.

All children are protected by a guardian angel until they reach the age of accountability, then it is up to them to call upon their angel if they wish.

Angels have rankings. There are prince angels, guardian angels, leaders and archangels. Archangels are the most powerful of all the angels.

Your child's imaginary friend may well be an angel.

Evidence says that children not only hear angels but may be more likely to see them than adults.

Angels never die. They are immortal beings.

Not all angels appear to have wings. Some have manifested as human beings.

How To Make Your Own Set of Angel Cards

We all want to know what the future holds for us and one of the best tools for divination are angel cards, but they can work out expensive to buy. Below we show you how to make your very own set of angel oracle cards...

You will need

27 pieces of card approximately 7cm x 11cm (plain or coloured)

A pencil

Some coloured pens

An A4 sheet of paper to copy out the meanings

Optional – a laminating machine to laminate your cards

This is a very creative project where you can let your imagination run wild! Look at the angel meanings below and draw and colour in a picture that you feel depicts the meaning of that card. Write the name of the angel below your picture. If you don't feel very creative, you can always find images on Google Images or from magazines.

Angels and their meanings

Angel of Hope: There is light at the end of the tunnel. Your angel of hope is telling you that things are moving in the right direction. Use the power of hope to make all your dreams come true.

Angel of Abundance: Your prayers will soon be answered. The angel of abundance surrounds you and will be sending you gifts very soon.

Angel of Strength: You do have the strength to see this through. The angel of strength gives you the power to see a situation through to completion.

Angel of Peace: The angel of peace asks you to sit still for a while and let the peace flood into your life.

Angel of Forgiveness: The angel of forgiveness urges you to forgive yourself and others. Holding on to a grudge will eat you up inside.

Angel of Patience: Now is not the time to start something new. Wait and bide your time.

Angel of Truth: Honesty is always the best policy. Be honest and true with yourself and others.

Angel of Balance: Balance all the areas in your life now to keep harmony and peace in your life.

Angel of Faith: Have faith that all your dreams will come true – Rome wasn't built in a day, you know.

Angel of Joy: Joy is all around you. Stop for a moment to appreciate it.

Angel of Inspiration: New ideas are being sent to inspire you. Listen and take note.

Angel of Love: The angel of love is reminding you that love is all around you. Express and embrace it.

Angel of Courage: The angel of courage is telling you that you can do it and is giving you the strength to beat any obstacles. Go for it.

Angel of Creativity: Think you're not creative? Think again. The angel of creativity is sending you the message to get creative. You don't know where it might lead.

Angel of Communications: Look out for emails, messages of synchronicity and new people because the angel of communications is working with you.

Angel of Relationships: The angel of relationships is giving you the strength to express yourself in all your relationships.

Angel of Trust: Trust is paramount in any relationship. This angel is telling you to trust in others and in yourself.

Angel of Happiness: You can be happy, you just need to give yourself permission to be happy.

Angel of Fun: Bogged down by life? The angel of fun is encouraging you to go play again. Become a child and learn how to have fun.

Angel of Blessings: We should all take time to reflect and count our blessings. The angel of blessings is telling you to count yours.

Angel of Judgement: Try not to judge another person unless you have walked a mile in their shoes.

Angel of Happiness: Happiness is yours for the taking; you just have to ask for it from the angels and it will be there.

Angel of Gratitude: Be grateful for what you do have in your life right now and you will soon have more to be grateful for.

Angel of Healing: The angel of healing will help you to heal from the inside out. Once you ask you will soon be fighting fit mentally and physically.

Angel of Comfort: Take comfort now that the angels are looking after you. Sometimes we have to put up with the rain in order to see the rainbow.

Angel of Prosperity: Prosperity isn't all about money; it's about your life as a whole. This angel is about to bring you the lot.

Angel of Luck: This angel will bring you lots of luck that you have never experienced before. Look out for the signs.

A Simple Angel Oracle Reading
Find a quiet place where you won't be disturbed. Light a white tea-light candle and shuffle your personalised set of Angel Oracle cards. Think of a question that you would like to be answered.

Take out three cards to represent your past, three to represent the present, three to represent your future and one more card to represent the whole outcome.

Turn over each card in turn and read the message of each card.

The 10 cards should give you an overall view on what you should do, and remember to always thank your angels for helping you.

How to Connect With Your Angel
As said before, we all have a guardian angel. Some people have

several that look out for us on a daily basis. Many of our past relatives or friends become our guardian angels and look after us as they would have done when they were here living on earth. Signs that your guardian angel is one of your friends or relatives is that their favourite song comes on the radio when you are thinking about them, or you see their name all the time in magazines or books, or you find white feathers in unusual places whenever you think about them. You may even hear their voice just as you are about to go to sleep. If you feel that someone you know who has passed could be your guardian angel, ask them to show you a sign – and they will.

Others have guardian angels that are not related, but are assigned to us from birth. Again, if you want to know their name, ask them. They will let you know by showing you their name somewhere, or a name might just pop into your head. If it does, ask your guardian angel by name to give you confirmation by way of a sign. Once you have asked for a sign, or for help, don't dwell on it. Just be assured that someone 'up there' is listening to you and that things will happen and that your problems will be solved.

Make Your Own Guardian Angel

You can make your own guardian angel very easily, which will protect you and your home/office.

You will need:

A lump of quick-dry modelling clay.
A pinch of dried sage.
A pink candle.
A lighter or matches.
A pinch of salt.
A saucer.

Decide where you want your angel to sit and watch over you.

Split your modelling clay into eight equal parts. Roll one part into a ball for your angel's head – you can mark on eyes and a smile if you wish. Roll the other bits of clay to make a body, two legs, two arms and of course, two wings. Stick them all together to create your guardian angel.

Put your guardian angel figure on a saucer and place the pink candle behind the figure. Sprinkle a circle of salt and a circle of dried sage around your figure and candle. Light your candle and say the following:

> *'Guardian angel, may you protect me and my home (office)*
> *And fill my life with love and happiness.'*

Allow the candle to burn down safely and allow your angel figure to dry. Once dried, you can put your guardian angel wherever you like. You can make a mini one to go in your bag or in your car, if you wish.

Numerology

Numerology originated from a Greek maths genius called Pythagoras, who lived thousands of years ago – think a Greek version of Carol Vorderman. It's basically the study of numbers and the way in which certain numbers can tell you about the character of a person, what their purpose in life will be and where their talents lie. Numerology experts are often employed to give financial forecasts to businesses, as well as to predict some of our most important decisions in life, such as, when to get married, when to move house and what job we should be doing.

Many fortune-telling divinations are dismissed by scientists and academics as ridiculous because they can't be proved by science. Numerology is more accepted by cynics of divination systems, because we're dealing with numbers and numbers feature heavily in science and academia.

NAME NUMBERS

Over the years there have been lots of different numerology systems. One of the easiest ones to do to find out what a person is like, is to work out their name number. To do this you need to find out their full birth name. Nicknames, names changed by marriage or Deed Poll do not count. It's only *full birth names* that count. Each letter in a person's name represents a number. Those numbers are all added together to eventually reach a single number, which is that person's name number.

Below is an example:

Gemma Holly Granger

1	2	3	4	5	6	7	8	9
A	B	C	D	E	F	G	H	I
J	K	L	M	N	O	P	Q	R
S	T	U	V	W	X	Y	Z	

For Gemma's first name the numbers corresponding with the letters in her name are as follows:

G = 7

E = 5

M = 4

M= 4

A = 1

So Gemma's first name in numerology looks like this:

7 + 5 + 4 + 4 + 1 = 21

2 + 1 = 3

Her middle name is as follows:

H = 8

O = 6

L = 3

L = 3

Y = 7

8 + 6 + 3 + 3 + 7 = 27

2 + 7 = 9

Finally Gemma's surname is as follows:

G = 7

R = 9

A = 1

N = 5

G = 7

E = 5

R = 9

So her surname looks like this:

7 + 9 + 1 + 5 + 7 + 5 + 9 = 43

4 + 3 = 7

Add all the three final numbers together from Gemma's full name – in this case, **3, 9 and 7** which come to **19**. Now you need to get this number down to a single number, so you add the **1** and **9** together, which gives you **10** (still a double figure number). Now add the **1** and the **0** together, which gives you a final number of **1**.

So Gemma's name number is 1.
Try this with your own name and see what number you get. Look below at the personality traits for birth numbers.

Number 1
An inventor of ideas, strong leadership skills, independent, driven, aggressive, boastful.

Number 2
Cooperative, adaptable, sensitive, spiritual, shy, fearful, self-conscious.

Number 3
Imaginative, artistic, happy, fun-loving, scatty, lack of direction, self-centred.

Number 4
Strong values, family orientated, practical, scientific, attention to detail, stubborn, serious.

Number 5
Visionary, quick thinking, curious, exploring, restless, impatient.

Number 6
Responsible, artistic, nurturing, sympathetic, self-righteous, outspoken.

Number 7
Skilled, analytical, intelligent, scientific, argumentative,

sarcastic.

Number 8

Political, authoritative, decisive, powerful, impatient, material-istic.

Number 9

Friendly, selflessness, obliging, possessive, attention seeking.

So, Gemma's birth analysis according to numerology is that she is a strong person, with good ideas. She is independent and driven, but can have a tendency to be aggressive and boastful at times.

BIRTHDAY NUMBERS

Your date of birth can reveal a lot about yourself and others. In basic numerology, a numerologist will look at not only your name, but your date of birth when working out your life-path numerological forecast.

Look at the list below and see what date you were born:

1st of the month

Number 1 is an energy number and gives you leadership qualities, which indicates that you will make a good leader/manager/people person. You are powerful and have an air of self-confidence about you, but you can also be rather sensitive and keep your feelings to yourself.

2nd of the month

You are sensitive and emotional, but have great intuition. Number twos are very social people, but can feel nervous in large groups. You're a warm-hearted and caring person who needs to be loved. You can be prone to depression.

3rd of the month
Number threes have bags of energy and you always bounce back from any problems or challenges life throws at you. You have an easy nature but this can sometimes seem as though you don't care. You are good with words and make an excellent writer.

4th of the month
You are a born organiser and love nothing more that sorting people out. You're honest and reliable and make a wonderful employee. You sometimes repress your feelings and find it hard to show your affection at times. You can also be a bit stubborn when you want to be.

5th of the month
With a birthday on the 5th of the month you are inclined to work well with people and enjoy them. You are talented and versatile, very good at presenting ideas. You may have a tendency to get itchy feet at times and need change and travel. Sometimes you shy away from responsibility.

6th of the month
You're one of the most helpful and understanding numbers in numerology. You are also one of the most honest. Your life tends to centre around other people and this makes you a good counsellor/social worker or mentor.

7th of the month
You are a perfectionist and like to be different from everyone else. You are often psychic and find that you empathise with people easily. You listen to your gut instincts, which are always right. You don't like to take orders from others though.

8th of the month
Born on the 8th day of the month, you have a special gift for

business, as you can conceive and plan on a grand scale. You have good executive skills and you're a good judge of values. You should try to own your own business, because you have such a strong desire to be in control. This number is associated with material success.

9th of the month
Your birth on the 9th day of the month adds a tone of idealism and humanitarianism to your nature. You become one who can work easily with people because you are broad-minded, tolerant and generous. You are ever sensitive to others' needs and feelings, and can sympathise with them easily.

10th of the month
You are independent and don't like to rely on others too much. You have great leadership qualities and self-confidence. You don't care too much about what others think of you and tend to live a life to your own rules, rather than those of others.

11th of the month
Your birth on the 11th day of the month makes you something of a dreamer and an idealist. You work well with people because you know how to use persuasion rather than force. There is a strong spiritual side to your nature, and are sensitive, though often temperamental.

12th of the month
Being born on the 12th day of the month is likely to add a good bit of vitality to your life. You can be restless and looking for adventure, but you have a 'couldn't care less' attitude sometimes. You excel in writing, speaking, and possibly singing. You are energetic and always a good conversationalist. You have a keen imagination, but you tend to scatter your energies.

13th of the month

Being born on the 13th day of the month should help make you a better manager and organiser, but it may also give you a tendency to dominate people a bit. You are responsible and self-disciplined, as well as honest and serious about your work. You can, however, become intolerant to people who do not pull their weight.

14th of the month

You are inclined to work well with people and enjoy them. You are talented and versatile, very good at presenting ideas, and you are also very good at organisation. You may have a tendency to get itchy feet at times and need change and travel. You can become restless and bored easily.

15th of the month

With a birthday on the 15th of any month, you are very close to your home and family life. People born on the 15th day of the month are excellent teachers, parents or mentors. You love to pass information on to others. You also love to learn new things and make great cooks or artists. Generous to a fault, but you can also be stubborn.

16th of the month

Those born on the 16th of the month tend to be loners. You're independent and like to do things at your own pace. You can have trouble finding the right life partner, but once you have found him/her, you will stay together forever. You dance to your own tune, so your dress sense can be a bit unusual. You are also very intuitive.

17th of the month

Those born on the 17th of the month can expect a fortunate life with regards to finances. You have a good head for business and often start your own empires that do well financially. You are an excellent organiser and your natural sensitivity makes you a great boss. You sometimes find it hard to accept compliments though.

18th of the month

Your birthday on the 18th day of the month suggests than you are one who can work well with a group, but still remain someone who needs to maintain your own identity. You make a good campaigner and have a lot of tolerance. You are also one of the most broad-minded people, so very little shocks you. You prefer to give than receive.

19th of the month

You're an independent person with bags of energy. You have leadership qualities second to none and enjoy sorting other people out. You also have an air of confidence about you. This can sometimes be taken as arrogance though by others. You tend not to follow the crowd and do your own thing and you try not to be influenced by other people.

20th of the month

Your birth on the 20th day of the month adds a degree of emotion, sensitivity, and intuition to your character. You are very social and make friends easily, but you can also feel nervous in large groups where you don't know anyone. You can be moody at times if things don't go your way, but these feelings rarely last very long.

21st of the month

You are one of the most easy-going people and couldn't really care less about what people think of you. You love to sing and many 21st-born people do become professional singers or actors. You have a good imagination, but this can scatter your energies sometimes, meaning you can forget important dates or meetings. You are very affectionate and loyal.

22nd of the month
You can be stubborn and won't take no for an answer. You are also one hard worker and will be the one last to leave the office and first back in in the morning. You are at your best when you are organising a project or an event, but you can forget to look after yourself and eat properly. You are also prone to nervous tension and anxiety.

23rd of the month
Those born on 23rd are people persons. You love to socialise and enjoy meeting new people and you probably have tons of friends to hang out with. You also love travel and don't like to be tied to one place for too long. You can get restless and bored easily, so you need new things constantly to keep you busy. You do have a tendency to sulk if you don't get your own way.

24th of the month
If you were born on 24th you a one of life's helpers and love nothing more than to help others. You are the peacemaker of the family and the one everyone turns to for advice or just to sound off to. Your family and their happiness is the most important thing to you. You are also one of the most affectionate of people, not afraid to wear your heart on your sleeve.

25th of the month
If you were born on 25th you are one of those people that love technology and all things a little bit sciency. You would have excelled in maths or science subjects and are fascinated by space and the unknown. I'll bet you love sci-fi too! Your thinking is logical and you analyse situations before committing to anything. You would make a great inventor or computer wizard.

26th of the month

Those born on 26th of the month often succeed in business well. You handle problems well and can often foresee things that others can't before they have happened. You are ambitious and handle money well. You are also very diplomatic and can see both sides of an argument. You are practical and these skills come in handy in everyday life.

27th of the month

You are selfless and always put others' happiness before yourself. You are one of the most generous of people and will work all hours to help other people out if you have to. You are also very broad-minded and have a 'live and let live' attitude to life. Not much shocks you and you are very sensitive and understanding to other people, regardless of how they choose to live their lives.

28th of the month

Being born on 28th of the month makes you one of the most confident people. You are original and unique and don't like to put people into boxes. You work well with figures and like solving problems. You have good leadership qualities and would never leave a job unfinished, no matter how boring it is. You see the good in everyone and are one of the most forgiving people.

29th of the month

You are imaginative and creative, but rather uncomfortable in the business world. You are very aware and sensitive, with outstanding intuitive skills and analytical abilities. You can suffer from nervous tension. This is the birthday of the dreamer rather than the doer. You do, however, work very well with people.

30th of the of the month

If you are born on 30th of the month you are an expressive person who likes to be liked. You can be very dramatic and would make a good actor or presenter. You also have a very vivid imagination, which makes you ideal as a natural storyteller or writer. You can be a bit messy in your surroundings, but this is only because you have other things to be getting on with.

31st of the month

Those born at the very end of the month are good organisers and can be depended on to sort things out. You are patient and have determination. These skills come in handy in the world of business. You are good with details and accuracy. You love travel, but wouldn't travel on your own because you like company.

LIFE PATH NUMBERS

Your Life Path number is the total sum of your birth date. This number represents who you are at the time of your birth and highlights your natural positive and negative traits that will remain with you throughout your life journey.

The Life Path number is established by taking the numbers from the date you were born, the month and the year, adding them together until you get a single digit.

For example: if you were born on 27th October 1986, the numbers you would add together would be as such:

$2 + 7 + 1 + 0 + 1 + 9 + 8 + 6 = 34$.

$3 + 4 =$ **a Life Path number of 7**

Read about your Life Path Number below:

Numerology Life Path 1

The Life Path number one people usually make good leaders. You are independent and reach goals easily. Many political leaders or entrepreneurs are number one people. You are very good at getting projects off the ground and have a good eye for detail than many others miss. You're at your best when there are problems or challenges to overcome and you have a determination to get to the bottom of things.

Number one people are often inventors. You don't like routine too much and like to be kept busy with different things going on in your life all the time. You are very ambitious and social, but you can come across as a bit self-centred to those who don't know you. You don't handle rejection or disapproval well. You will find that other number one people will be drawn to you, but this can cause problems in relationships with the struggle to be the most dominant one.

You work better as a leader than a follower, but you may have to learn to climb the ladder to success by taking orders for a while, so avoid being too bossy to those who know a bit more than you.

Numerology Life Path 2

The Life Path 2 suggests that you are a very spiritual person and are one of life's peacemakers. You have excellent listening skills and will often find yourself being a mediator to others. You are diplomatic and would never intentionally upset or hurt anyone. You are the person other people turn to in times of need.

You appear to have an inner strength that is alien to many others, but you can be prone to thinking of others' needs far more than your own, resulting in stress and feeling out of balance sometimes. You can often see both sides of an argument and can be unbiased when it comes to taking sides. You like good manners and like everyone around you to be having a good time. If you see someone is being left out, you will be the first to step in and offer the hand of friendship.

You like routine and familiarity and can get tense if there are sudden changes in your life. You also have a habit of overanalysing things. You have many ideas, but are often so busy making sure that others are OK that you put your goals to one side, in the hope that one day you will find the time to dedicate to yourself.

Two's often struggle with making decisions and will leave things to the last minute rather than jump into something that might be wrong for them.

Numerology Life Path 3

The Life Path 3 indicates that you are a good communicator and achievement comes easily to you. You have exceptional communication skills and excel in anything to do with public services, writing or journalism. Number three people are entertainers and very often go into acting or show business.

You live life to the full and have the philosophy that life really is for living. If you have money in your pocket you will spend it all, which can be a problem if you have to stick to a budget. You are very generous and like to treat people, worrying about tomorrow when it comes.

You connect well with people from all walks of life and are one of the most sociable people on the planet. You make people feel at home and are the first to start a conversation if no one else is prepared to speak first.

You are surprisingly sensitive and can retreat into your shell from time to time. This doesn't last long though and you soon come bouncing back from any knockbacks.

Numerology Life Path 4

Being a Life Path 4 means you are a natural fixer. You are down to earth and practical and if something needs fixing in life, you are the person to call on. You are one of those naturally talented people who can turn their hand to anything and will achieve success, fame or both throughout your life.

You are good at taking orders and will happily work all hours to see a job finished. You make an excellent manager or boss and are probably involved with your community in some way. You have a stubbornness about you, but this is seen as a positive, rather than a negative. Once you make a decision, you will stick to it, regardless of whether or not it is right or wrong.

You are a born organiser and a perfectionist and make one of the most loyal of friends, but sometimes you can be so organised that you forget to look up and see what's going on around you. Friendships are with a few select, but they will be for life.

People tend to lean on you a lot, but can sometimes get too involved with other people's problems. Don't get involved too much.

Numerology Life Path 5

If you were born with a Life Path number of 5, it suggests that you are a person who wants to make the world a better place. You make a great campaigner and a creator of change for the better.

You were born for adventure and love freedom. You're also a huge supporter of the underdog and will do anything to help those who can't help themselves. You do well in local politics and excel at debates.

Any job where you have to communicate with others is ideal for you; this includes sales and marketing, because you have a way with people that makes them feel relaxed and comfortable with you.

Because of your love for adventure, you do get bored easily and hate routine. Your happy-go-lucky nature may drive others mad, but you really do live for the day and leave the worrying up to other people.

You don't like to be tied down or restricted, so need a relationship with someone who understands that you like your own space and someone who doesn't get jealous.

Numerology Life Path 6

As a number six, you are one of life's caretakers and love nothing more than to look after others. You like truth and justice and are one of the most maternal people on the planet. If you have a family, you quickly become the 'glue' that holds everything together.

You are usually happy and are supportive to those who need a pick-me-up. You're ideal life is one of domesticity and love nothing more than making people feel at home. You make a good leader and take your responsibilities in life very seriously. The only downfall of this is that people can often take advantage of your good nature.

In romance you are very loyal and will look after your partner's needs more than your own. You don't like conflict and try to smooth things over if an argument breaks out and will always be the first to back down and say sorry, even if you are not at fault.

You are compassionate and trustworthy, but can come across as a bit controlling at times. This is only because you want everyone to be happy in life. You and rejection don't mix well and you get easily hurt if someone doesn't accept your help.

Numerology Life Path 7

Someone born with the Life Path number 7 is a deep thinker who will analyse everything to death. You set yourself very high standards and come across as a bit of perfectionist in life. You are full of questions and will often question the motives of other people. These skills means that you rarely get taken for a ride, because you are so cautious. However, this can sometimes be difficult for other people who don't have an agenda or a game plan.

You make a good comedian thanks to your natural wit and you can charm the birds out of the trees with your charming personality. Chances are you have a lot of friends and a good social life, but can sometimes come across as a bit aloof with people you don't know very well. This is only because you don't trust people as easily as others.

You enjoy your own company and can happily sit in a

crowded room and not talk to a soul, if the mood takes you. You don't care what people think of you and are intolerant of others' opinions if they don't match your own.

The number seven is a very spiritual number, so it wouldn't surprise me if you were a bit psychic. Regardless, you will investigate different spiritual practices to discover which one suits you the most.

Number seven's often prefer to live alone because their tolerance levels can be low at times and they need their own space.

Numerology Life Path 8

You are a natural leader if you are a number eight and you like to organise people. You're very ambitious and goal-oriented and quietly climb the ladder to success.

You are also an ideas person and will carve out a niche for doing something different in life. You have the potential to go far. It might take a while to get where you want to be – but you will get there. You are very independent and don't like to rely on others too much.

You would make a good manager, executive or entrepreneur and your ability to make good character judgements is excellent. You enjoy recognition for your hard work and with that comes money and power.

In relationships you are direct and honest. You never wear your heart on your sleeve and rarely show your affection. People often mistake your enthusiasm for bossiness.

Numerology Life Path 9

If you were born under the number nine, you are one dramatic soul! Drama seems to follow you wherever you go and you would do well in show business or a career as an actor. You are naturally generous and compassionate with others and have a great empathy with people from all walks of life.

Material things don't interest you much and you have a good attitude to money – if you have it, you'll spend it; if you don't, it won't be a big deal to you. You are selfless and would happily share anything with anyone. Because of this, you make friends easily.

You're very open to people and others warm to you. Relationships are sometimes difficult because people can take advantage of you, if you're not careful.

You're quite a sensitive soul at heart but will find that you can channel this through painting, signing, writing, or other creative avenues. Number nine's often feel sad at the state of the world and find themselves asking why people can't just get along. You would make a good charity fundraiser or campaigner.

Numerology is a great way of finding out who you are and who you are most compatible with. Science and folklore have come a long way. If you have an iPhone or iPad, you can now download numerology Apps that will calculate your personality numbers and those of your friends, lovers and anyone else for that matter.

Crystal Readings

Crystals are one of nature's most amazing creations. They also look fabulous on nails and equally fabulous in jewellery. Crystals are formed naturally over time, when tiny molecules form to create specific shapes. Some crystals you will already know, such as salt, sugar and ice – all tiny naturally produced crystals. Crystals are used in many things we use today – computers, watches and radios, all have quartz crystals inside them. They are also natural energy conductors so are ideal for use in alternative healing.

There are many different types of crystals and the more we learn about the earth, the more are being discovered on and beneath our planet.

Crystal reading or crysallomancy as it is correctly known, has been around almost as long as the crystals themselves and has always been an accurate way of predicting the fortunes of people or guiding them in the right direction for their true path. Readings are usually done using smooth, small gemstones.

Below I outline some of the most common crystals that you can buy in New Age shops today and show you how to do your own crystal readings:

Amazonite

Amazonite is a beautiful greeny-blue gemstone, also known as microcline. If this stone is picked in a reading it signals new adventures, projects or new starts. Life is about to show you that getting out there and trying new things will lead to great opportunities.

Amethyst

The Amethyst stone is very common and is part of the quartz family of crystals. It is usually purple or lilac in colour. If you pick this stone it is telling you to use your imagination in a bid to get your goals.

Aquamarine

This gemstone is, as the name suggests, connected to the sea. It looks almost transparent, like ice. This stone when picked in a reading is warning you to be careful of gossip. Don't listen to others until you have all the facts.

Aventurine

This beautiful stone looks like an emerald, but it has sparkles inside it. When you pick this stone it is a sign that you are about to start on a new venture. Known also as the gambler's stone, this gem will bring you luck in lotteries.

Azurite

This electric-blue stone is both rare and beautiful and tells of psychic abilities. It also tells you that a situation will soon be resolved to your satisfaction. Use this stone if you need some healing.

Bloodstone

So called due to the small particles of iron inside the stone, the Bloodstone is another member of the quartz family. This is telling you to persevere because things are about to get better for you.

Blue Lace Agate

Blue Lace Agate is another member of the quartz family and is white in colour, with a hint of blue. You can expect news coming to you soon in the form of a text, email or phone call. This is the gem of communication.

Carnelian

This smooth orange stone is also known as Sard. By choosing this gemstone you are being told that balance will soon be restored and that stressful situations will soon be a distant memory.

Citrine

So called because of its lemon colour, this rare stone brings prosperity and joy into your life. If things have been a bit difficult recently, picking this gemstone tells you that things are about to improve.

Clear Quartz

Clear Quartz, otherwise known as Rock Crystal, is the purest form of the mineral silicon dioxide and is almost transparent in appearance. This stone is encouraging you to focus on your goals because success is close by.

Jasper

Jasper is a brown/orange coloured stone and folklore states that it would protect a man from being bitten by a snake. When you pick this stone it is telling you to stop wasting time on those who don't appreciate you. Concentrate on yourself and your dreams.

Labradorite

This beautiful blue gemstone is also known as the magic stone. Changes are ahead for you and they will be very positive. Be careful to think about what it is you want, because you will get it.

Lapis Lazuli

This gemstone is deep blue with tiny flecks of gold and silver throughout it. This is the stone of studying and is advising you to go back to school and learn more. You may have to research something in order to go to the next level.

Lepidolite

Lepidolite is a light purple gemstone that comes from lithium. It is telling you to stop beating yourself up and to forgive yourself. The past is in the past now; move on.

Malachite

This green stone is said to protect you from the evil eye. Forgiveness is the greatest gift you can have. Don't bear grudges because you will find it hard to move on. Forgive those who have upset you and you will feel better because of it.

Milky Quartz

This stone is so called because of its milky appearance and is part of the quartz family. You are being told to wait and do nothing for the moment. The situation will be resolved naturally.

Moonstone

This gemstone looks almost like a pearl with its bluey/white finish. This is the stone of patience and is telling you to wait a while before committing yourself to anything. Things will soon be sorted out.

Obsidian

Obsidian is a form of natural glass and was often used to make mirrors. Picking this stone suggests that things have been a bit turbulent in your life recently. Change is on the cards but you are being told to expect the unexpected.

Peacock Ore

Also known as Bornite, this stone brings you good luck and contentment. This happy little stone is full of joy. There may also be news of a pregnancy.

Pyrite

Pyrite is also known as Fool's Gold. This gemstone is warning you not to be taken for a fool. Things are not what they first seems so don't believe everything you hear.

Rose Quartz

Rose Quartz is a rare stone from the quartz family and this pink gem is connected to love and friendships in your life. Love is in the air, so expect plenty of admirers. Rose Quartz will also protect your computer from viruses if you place one nearby.

Rutilated Quartz

Another member of the quartz family, which is transparent with fine golden hairs running through it. This suggests you should look to a group of people to help you with a problem. Don't try to do things all on your own.

Selenite

This crystal looks like glass and suggests that you need to be prepared for challenges ahead. There may be a temporary separation from someone, but it won't be for long.

Smokey Quartz

This stone looks like a piece of burned coal and brings a feeling of calmness and clarity to your life. You may feel as though things are taking ages to happen, but be patient because things are about to change for the better.

Schorl

When heated, this stone is charged positive and negative at the same time. This is the stone for the traveller and suggests that you may be travelling to another country soon. This stone is said to relieve jet leg.

Tiger's Eye

So called because of the tiger-like strips within this stone, this gem brings good luck to the wearer and suggests that success is on the way to you. Your confidence will grow because of this.

Topaz

This beautiful blue stone can be found in other colours, including; yellow, orange, brown and clear. Choosing this gemstone shows a leadership quality. You will inspire others around you, but don't become too bossy!

Turquoise

The Turquoise stone is blue, but absorbs dirt and oils, which gives it a veiny look. This stone is telling you to take care of your health. It also suggests that you are psychic and should look into this gift further.

Whilst you don't need all 28 gemstones to do a crystal reading, if you can get the 28 stones, all the better. For an effective reading, you should have at least 12 of the above gemstones.

Doing a Crystal Reading

Your gemstones should all be around the same size and you will need a small pouch or bag to put keep them in.

When doing a reading, it's always best to light a white candle or tea-light to clear the air of any negativity.

To begin your reading, swirl your hand inside your crystal bag so as to mix up the stones. The following format is for a general crystal reading. Pick one crystal for each area:

Crystal 1 Your personal life at the moment
Crystal 2 Your finances at the moment
Crystal 3 Communications
Crystal 4 Home and family issues
Crystal 5 Children
Crystal 6 Work, career issues
Crystal 7 Relationships, romance

Crystal 8 Finances, prosperity
Crystal 9 Travel
Crystal 10 The near future
Crystal 11 Challenges
Crystal 12 The outcome to your questions

If you wish to do a reading for a specific area in your life, use the following technique for any question:

Crystal 1 The recent past
Crystal 2 The present
Crystal 3 The near future
Crystal 4 The future
Crystal 5 The final outcome

Obviously, as with all divination readings, they can't be completely specific to your question, so you do need to use your intuition and common sense to answer a specific question. For example; if you were questioning the state of your love life and you drew the Topaz stone for your final outcome, it would suggest that you need to be less domineering in your relationship.

Below is a sample crystal reading using the specific area reading for Chloe who wants to know whether she should move in with her boyfriend or go travelling with her best friend.

Crystal One

Selenite – This stone is relating to Chloe's recent past and suggests that she is about to make an important decision. She realises that she will have to make a decision, which will have challenges with other people (in this case her boyfriend or her best friend).

Crystal Two

Tiger's Eye – Chloe is more confident than she realises and Lady Luck is shining on her at the moment.

Crystal Three

Pyrite – Chloe is being warned that everything may not be as it seems. Before she commits to anything, she must do her research and look into both situations thoroughly.

Crystal Four

Jasper – this suggests that Chloe may find settling down with her boyfriend will tie her down before she's ready. She needs to follow her own dreams before putting anyone else before her.

Crystal Five

Schorl – This stone is the traveller's stone and suggests that Chloe should go travelling with her best friend for a while before settling down with her boyfriend. She should go for her goals.

As with all forms of divination, nothing is set in stone. All divinations act as guides and suggest what the outcome will be. If Chloe decided to stay with her boyfriend then that is her own free will. Although the above reading suggests that she would be better off travelling, at the end of the day, it is ultimately Chloe's decision as to what to do.

As with all fortune-telling systems, the more you practise, the better you will become at giving readings. If you can't find the exact crystals, buy the ones that you are most drawn to.

Crystals in Healing

It's not just in divination that crystals can help you: crystals can help with your health too. Below is a short list of crystals and how they can help heal you:

Healing Crystal

Addictions: Kunzite or Lepidolite

Nightmares: Jet, Ruby or Celestite

Stress: Amethyst, Sodalite or Celestite

Emotional Stress: Malachite or Peridot

Anger: Sapphire, Ruby or Bloodstone

Anxiety: Emerald, Smithsonite or Kunzite

Depression: Jet, Sunstone or Kunzite

Fear: Rose Quartz

Panic Attacks: Smithsonite or Kunzite

Menstruation: Garnet or Carnelian

Blisters: Rose Quartz

Hayfever: Jet or Blue Lace Agate

Ulcers: Fluorite or Peridot

Aches and Pains: Spinel

Asthma: Amber or Topaz

Headaches: Amethyst

Back pain: Malachite, Hematite or Lapis

High blood pressure: Amethyst or Bloodstone

Acne: Amethyst

For crystal healing either carry the appropriate crystal in your pocket or wear as a necklace, or you can put the crystal in your bath and soak up the healing energies. Crystals are not an alternative to conventional medicine, so if symptoms persist please go and see your GP.

I-CHING

The I-Ching is China's oldest method of divining the future and came from an ancient text called *The Book of Changes*. This old system is at the heart of Chinese culture and its philosophy is based around balance and the acceptance of change in order for our lives to become balanced and harmonious.

There are many complicated methods of the I-Ching using

various tools, but the method we are going to look at here is a basic form of I-Ching, involving the use of three coins. It helps if the three coins are of the same denomination (three pound-coins, for example).

As well as your three coins, you will need a pen/pencil and a piece of paper.

How to do an I-Ching reading...

Think of a question you would like some guidance on and hold the three coins in your most dominant hand. Give them a little shake.

Throw all three coins down onto a table at the same time.

Record the coins as to whether they land heads up or tails up as follows:

Each coin that lands heads up equals the number 3

Each coin that lands tails up equals the number 2

So, if for example, you have two heads and one tail it will equal:

3 + 3 + 2

This will give you a total of 8 for your first throw.

To translate this into an I-Ching reading you need to draw a line that will indicate your first throw came to an eight. As below:

The number 8 is represented as a broken line like this:

_____ _____

The combinations you will get from throwing your three coins can be:

3 heads = 9 = _____ (one long line)
2 heads and 1 tail = 8 = _____ _____ (a broken line)
1 head and 2 tails = 7 = _____ (one long line)
3 tails = 6 = _____ _____ (a broken line)

Repeat this process five more times – throw the coins, make a note of their total value and draw the relevant line down on a piece of paper.

So for example:

Your first throw results in 3 heads, which when added up equal 9, so your first line will be one long line. Your second throw results in 2 tails and 1 head, which equals 8, so your second line is a broken line. Your third throw results in 3 tails, which equals 6, so your third line is a broken line. Your fourth throw results in 3 heads, which equals another 9, so another unbroken line. Your fifth throw results in 1 head and 2 tails, which equals a 7, so your line will be an unbroken line and your sixth throw results in 1 head and 2 tails, which results in another 7, an unbroken line.

When you draw your lines start from the bottom upwards. So, if we were to draw the lines for the coin throws above, your I-Ching lines will look like this:

_____ total of 7 (6th throw)

_____ total of 7 (5th throw)

_____ total of 9 (4th throw) * changing line

_____ _____ total of 6 (3rd throw) *changing line

_____ _____ total of 8 (2nd throw)

_____ total of 9 (1st throw) * changing line

Easy enough, right? However, (here's the tricky bit), if you throw a total value of 9 or a 6, these are called Changing Lines, which I have marked with an asterisk for now. We will look at the Changing Lines a bit later.

Now to discover what your six lines mean: Every set of lines your coin throws make up will create what is known in the I-Ching as a hexagram. Below is a list of all the possible hexagram outcomes that you can have in an I-Ching reading and their meanings. Look at the table below to match your lines to the right one in the chart.

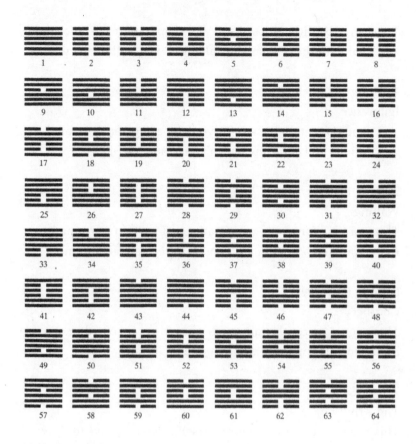

Name and Interpretation

1. Qián *(Force)*
The Creative
Progress is certain for success. Try not to be arrogant or you will lose sight of the success that is due to you

2. Kūn *(Field)*
The Receptive
Success will come, but only if you persevere. Be careful who you listen to and who you take advice from.

3. Chún *(Sprouting)*
Distress

There may be difficulties ahead, but if you are prepare for them and deal with them as small challenges, you will be the winner.

4. Méng *(Enveloping)*
Ignorance
You should listen to the advice you've been given now, but be a bit cautious that someone doesn't have a game plan.

5. Xū *(Attending)*
Waiting
This is a time for waiting and patience. Don't do anything in a rush. Wait and see what happens next before you rush in.

6. Sòng *(Arguing)*
Conflict
There could be conflict ahead. Try not to get involved in others' arguments. If you need advice, go to an expert.

7. Shī *(Leading)*
The Army
This is a time to stand up for yourself. You may have to show your leadership skills. Be careful because someone could be jealous of you.

8. Bi *(Grouping)*
Union
This is a peaceful and happy time. Don't doubt yourself that things will not work out; they will and with great results.

9. Xiao Chù *(Small Accumulating)*
Restraint
Take a step back and just watch and wait for a while. Patience is required now for you to get ahead.

10. **Lu** *(Treading)*
Cautiousness
Remain cautious for now. Good fortune is ahead for you, but only if you check the details. Don't sign any contracts without legal advice.

11. **Tài** *(Pervading)*
Peace
Good fortune is forecast as is a peaceful and happy time ahead. Extra money should come to you soon.

12. **Pi** *(Obstruction)*
Stagnation
A time of waiting patiently for things to progress. If a relationship has become stagnant, it's time to move on and start afresh.

13. **Tóng Rén** *(Concording People)*
Sharing
You will soon have some news to share. Marriage and babies are highlighted. You may be invited to join a new group.

14. **Dà You** *(Great Possessing)*
Great Wealth
Wealth is on the way. Your hard work is about to pay off. This could be a promotion, a new job. Don't become complacent though.

15. **Qiān**
Humility
If you need help from someone, don't be too proud to ask for it. A partnership will benefit you now.

16. **Yu** *(Humbling)*

Marketing Yourself

Now is the time to market or promote yourself. Opportunities will present themselves, so don't ignore them. Everything will go as you planned it.

17. Súi *(Following)*

Following

Go with the flow and appreciate the good fortune around you. Use this time to prepare for your future.

18. Gu *(Corrupting)*

Act Carefully

Now is not the time to make drastic decisions. Act carefully before you commit yourself to anyone. Are they trustworthy? You need to ask yourself.

19. Lín *(Nearing)*

Approach

Troubles will soon disappear if you act with kindness. You catch more flies with honey. Success and recognition is highlighted for you.

20. Guān *(Viewing)*

Contemplation

Now is the time to sit back and contemplate what has been happening lately. You could do with the support of others right now.

21. Shì Kè *(Gnawing Bite)*

Achievements

Act professionally and you will soon see how quickly you will progress with something that you have been wishing for.

22. Bì *(Adorning)*

Adornment
If you look and act like you're successful, you will attract success into your life. This is a successful time for you.

23. **Bō** *(Stripping)*
Splitting Apart
Let go of things that no longer serve you. The cycle of difficulties will then end. Patience is required, but soon you will see light at the end of the tunnel.

24. **Fù** *(Returning)*
Renewal
The change of the seasons brings renewal for you now. Any troubles or worries will soon melt away. Positive change is ahead.

25. **Wú Wàng** *(Without Embroiling)*
Freedom from Vanity
Now's the time to look inside for the guidance you need. Prepare for the unexpected. Avoid being greedy or asking for more than you need.

26. **Dà Chù** *(Great Accumulating)*
Taming Force
Hard work will bring you success very soon. Keep your head down and get on with it. The time will pass quickly and you will soon be able to say, 'I did it!'

27. **Yí** *(Swallowing)*
Nurturing
It's time to look after and nurture yourself. Think of number one for a change. It's your time to shine.

28. **Dà Guò** *(Great Exceeding)*

Excess
Your situation will improve soon, but only if you can be patient for a little while longer. Evaluate your own strengths and weaknesses.

29. Kan *(Gorge)*
The Abyss
Now is the time to wait and see what happens next. Only fools rush in. Let things happen in their own good time.

30. Lí *(Radiance)*
Brightness
Business ventures will bring success if your use your intelligence. Cooperate with someone who can help you attain your goals now.

31. Xián *(Conjoining)*
Attraction
Envy and jealousy do nothing but eat you up. Do not envy others. Be open to new commitments and help and protect those who are weaker.

32. Héng *(Persevering)*
Persistence
Allow things to happen in their own time. A difficult situation will soon end. Marriage or partnerships will become stronger.

33. Dùn *(Retiring)*
Withdrawal
Stand back and withdraw for a while. Watch what is going on behind the scenes. Others may try to take advantage of you. Avoid confrontation if you can.

34. Dà Zhuàng *(Great Invigorating)*

Power of the Great
Others will be influenced by you, so act wisely. A period of peace and good fortune is ahead of you now and success is on the way.

35. Jìn (Prospering)
Advancement
This is a good time for business ideas. Look for someone who might be able to help you out. Your dreams will come true soon.

36. Míng Yí (Brightness Hiding)
Darkening of the Light
Try not to become too downhearted. Be careful of who you trust right now and be patient. Things take time to come together.

37. Jiā Rén (Dwelling People)
The Family
Your family and home life will be important to you right now. Ask them for support if you're not getting it, but remember to respect those you live with.

38. Kuí (Polarising)
Opposition
If you can remain flexible now you will avoid fights and conflict. Look for ways to bring peace into your world. If someone is determined to upset you, walk away.

39. Jian (Limping)
Obstruction
If there are obstacles in your way, go round them. Learn from your past mistakes and you'll be just fine if you don't repeat them.

40. **Xiè** (*Taking Apart*)

Taking Apart

New opportunities are on the way for you, but you may have to deal with some difficulties first. Learn lessons, but life is too short for regrets.

41. **Sun** (*Diminishing*)

Decrease

Avoid overdoing it. Try to restrain yourself. If you feel you have to go out every night, perhaps there is something missing in your home life. Don't burn the candle at both ends.

42. **Yì** (*Augmenting*)

Gain

A time of good fortune is ahead of you. You may have to travel, but you will soon be sharing good fortune.

43. **Guài** (*Parting*)

Displacing

Legal action may be necessary. Face any problems head on and get a professional involved to help you. Act with truth and your outcome will be good.

44. **Gòu** (*Coupling*)

Encounter

Try not to be too influenced by other people. Remain honest and truthful and let your own personality shine through. You don't need to copy anyone else.

45. **Cuì** (*Clustering*)

Gathering

This is a time when you are going to have to dedicate yourself to a project if you are going to see the results. Be prepared for a testing time. Join a like-minded group for inspiration.

46. **Shēng** *(Ascending)*
Ascending
Move steadily onward and upward. Be prepared to work hard to get where you want to be and you will do so. Success and rewards will come soon.

47. **Kùn** *(Confining)*
Hardship
There could be hard times ahead for you, but if you prepare yourself for a battle, you will be in a good position to tackle anything right now. Be wary of someone lying to you.

48. **Jing** *(Welling)*
The Well
This is a time to listen to that little voice inside your head – she gives good advice!

49. **Gé** *(Skinning)*
Change
Change is ahead for you bringing with it good opportunities. Try not to resist change because you're frightened. You will see we need change to grow.

50. **Ding** *(Holding)*
The Cauldron
Material and spiritual success surround you now. Keep this in mind when you are starting new projects because they will be successful.

51. **Zhèn** *(Shake)*
Thunder
Prepare for stormy weather! There could be a sudden shock and upset, but this will be temporary and success will soon take its place. Be wary of a gossipy person.

52. Gèn *(Bound)*
Stillness
This isn't a time to take risks. Sit back and take notice of the things going on around you. Partners could be feeling a bit left out.

53. Jiàn *(Infiltrating)*
Gradual Progress
Slowly but surely you will move towards your goals, if you take your time over your plans.

54. Guī Mèi *(Converting the Maiden)*
Marriageable Maiden
Think about joining a club or organisation that interests you and your talents will shine through.

55. Fēng *(Abounding)*
Abundance
Good fortune, abundance and prosperity surround you. Enjoy them but also prepare for less exciting times.

56. Lu *(Sojourning)*
The Traveller
Travel is highlighted. This could be literally travelling to somewhere new, or it could be more in your mind.

57. Xùn *(Ground)*
Willing Submission
Don't be too pushy with someone who is only trying to help. Have patience and take baby steps to what you want to achieve.

58. Duì *(Open)*
Joy
A fabulous time ahead full of joy and happy times! Get sociable

and get out there and show everyone how great you really are.

59. Huàn *(Dispersing)*
Dispersal
Pay attention to the needs of others – it's not all about you, you know! Allow someone else to be in the spotlight.

60. Jié *(Articulating)*
Limitation
If you learn that you can't possibly know everything and that we all have limitations, you will be better able to ask questions and learn more.

61. Zhōng Fú *(Centre Conforming)*
Inner Truth
A time for looking deep inside yourself; and you will soon come up with the answers to life's questions.

62. Xiao Guò *(Small Exceeding)*
Excess of the Small
Now is a time to study. Knowledge is power and this will lead to success.

63. Jì Jì *(Already Fording)*
After Completion
Changes are ahead. Make sure you prepare yourself for what might just happen because then you will be in charge of any changes.

64. Wèi Jì *(Not Yet Fording)*
Before Completion
You may have some difficulties to overcome, but if you persevere and have a clear goal of where you want to be next, you will succeed.

Changing Lines

Occasionally your six-line hexagram will have Changing Lines in it – remember we talked about this at the beginning of the chapter, where if your coins result in a six or nine, you make a little asterisk mark on the line to lets you know that it's a Changing Line?

With a hexagram with Changing Lines, when you have completed your first reading, it's time to change that hexagram's Changing Lines to make a new hexagram. So in the example I gave you earlier, the original hexagram looked like this:

```
_____
_____
_____ *
_____ _____*
_____ _____
_____ *
```

Lines one, three and four were either a six or a nine so these are your Changing Lines. This means you need to change them from a broken line to a full line, or from a full line to a broken line. So based on the example we were looking at, your new hexagram will now look like this:

```
_____
_____
_____ _____
_____
_____ _____
_____ _____
```

The first hexagram shows that you created the number 42 hexagram, which means that good fortune is on its way to you. Once you have altered the hexagram for the Changing Lines, you reveal a new hexagram, which in this case is number 53 – slowly but surely you will move towards your goals, if you take your time over your plans. So your full reading is saying that if you take it steady and slowly, success and good fortune will come your way.

It's quite tricky to get your head round the art of the I-Ching divination system, but it's also one of those fortune-telling techniques that is easily learned once you get the hang of it. Keep practising and you will soon find that you will know what the meanings of the hexagrams are by just looking at them.

Pyromancy

Pyromancy was one of the earliest forms of divination and it is thought it originated in ancient Greece, but research suggests China also used this fortune-telling tool as far back as 10,000BC. More recently, the great prophet Nostradamus would often use Pyromancy to help him predict his visions of the future. So what is it and how do you do it?

What is Pyromancy?

Pyromancy comes from *Pyros* the Greek word for fire and *manteia* the Greek word for divination. So Pyromancy is the divination by the means of using fire. The idea is that you think of a question or a situation that you want resolved and you will find the answers in the flame of the fire. As strange as it sounds, it does work.

There are different types of Pyromancy too. The most basic is where the diviner observes the flames from a fire or a candle and looks for shapes within the flames. Alomancy is divination by salt being thrown into the fire. Capnomancy, is what happens when you use the smoke from the fire for a reading; and Botanomancy, is the divination by burning herbs or plants. You can use any or all of the above in Pyromancy readings.

Preparation

Important
It is very important that you take extra care with anything involving fire and please do not try this form of divination if you have had a few drinks, or unsupervised if you are under 18.

You can practise Pyromancy in an open fire in the garden if you wish, but make sure that the fire is not near to any trees or anything flammable. Alternatively, you can do this is an indoor fireplace, but please make sure that you have sufficient ventilation. Alternatively, you can simply use a candle.

Using an Open Fire

You will need:

A fire pit
Wood – preferably applewood or oak
Matches or a lighter
A small amount of silver glitter
Some small pieces of paper and a pen
Fire lighters
Always do this in a safe environment.

Light your fire pit and leave the fire to get established.

Sit by the fire and on each slip of paper write down one question you would like answered.

Once the fire is well established, throw a small handful of silver glitter into the fire. Read your first question out loud, fold the first slip of paper into three, close your eyes and throw the paper into the flames.

This is the important part: Don't take your eyes off the fire otherwise you could easily miss some signs. Concentrate on the question you asked and stare into the flames of the fire. To begin with it will probably look just like flames, but if you let your eyes gaze *through* the flames, you will begin to see shapes emerge from the flames. With any form of divination it is a tool for your intuition, so you're not going to get actual words coming out of the fire. It is up to you to interpret the images in the flames. For example; if you are asking whether or not your man is the right one for you, you may see the shape of a house within the flames, indicating yes and that you could be setting up home together. If on the other hand you saw a fierce dragon in the flames, this could suggest that the relationship will be volatile.

Repeat this as many times as you like and write down the signs you see in the flames so that you can refer back to them at a later date.

Using a Candle

Again, please be careful when doing fire readings and always do this in a safe environment and extinguish your candle when you have finished.

You will need:

A long white candle
Match or a lighter
A candle holder

This is a really simple and easy divination system to do. Find a time when you won't be disturbed. Turn off any artificial lighting in the room. Concentrate on the question you want answered and light your candle. Wait a few minutes and close your eyes. Open your eyes and look into the flame of the candle. You may see small shapes appear, but you may also see the flame grow in height. If it grows, this indicates a positive answer to your question. If the flame decreases in size, it indicates a no answer. If the candle spits, it can indicate that arguments will erupt surrounding your question.

For further clarification blow the candle out. If the smoke from the candle is black, it indicates a negative. If the smoke is grey or white, it is a positive sign. If the smoke travels up in a straight line, the answer is positive. If it travels in a squiggly line, it indicates that there is still work to be done before you get a positive answer.

Often, once the candle has been blown out and the smoke has gone, the wick will curl into a shape or a letter. Keep an eye out for signs of hearts or initials when asking questions about love because these are clues to who is the one for you.

The colour of the flame can tell you many things:

Orange: that you are psychic
Red: a passionate relationship
Blue: calm will be restored soon
Yellow: happy times are ahead
Purple: enlightenment
Green: jealousy

The Moon and You

Crooners have sung about it, astronomers have studied it, man has walked on it. I'm talking of course about the wondrous sight that is the moon.

The moon has had a powerful influence on our lives since time began. Did you know for instance that before we had weather reporters, our ancestors would study the moon's phases in order to determine the best time in which to plant their crops? Or that the word *lunatic* comes from the Latin word *luna* meaning full moon and coincidentally police have reported that crime increases during the period leading up to the full moon. Studies have also shown that suicides, crimes of arson, murder and robbery are just a few subjects that increase during the phase of the full moon.

Few people realise that the moon has a huge influence on our lives and if you follow the moon phases and plan your actions around them, you will soon discover that you can achieve great results and have everything you desire...

The Moon Phases

The moon orbits the earth, but doesn't actually cast any light of its own. The only reason we see the moon from earth is because of the light that the sun emits. The sun shines on the moon and this is why we can see it in the sky.

It takes a full 28 days for the moon to fully orbit the earth and during this time it goes through four main phases – the waxing moon, the full moon, the waning moon and the new moon.

It is during these phases that the moon has an effect on our daily lives and studies have shown that if we choose a time when the moon is in one of the appropriate phases for our requirements, we are more likely to succeed in our aspirations.

The Waxing Moon

When you look into the sky and the moon looks like a D shape, this is known as the waxing moon. It is believed that the waxing moon is the ideal time if you want something positive to happen in your life. For example, if you are looking for a new job, the waxing moon is the best time to arrange an interview. The waxing moon comes between 7 and 14 days after the new moon and it has been shown to be an auspicious time for success, courage, luck, health and friendship, so if you are looking for new friends, then join a club when the moon is in its waxing phase.

The Full Moon

Throughout history the full moon has always been considered to be a magical time and it is believed that as the moon grows from waxing to full, so too will the power you put into anything positive. Witches will often cast special positive spells on a full moon. Although there have been reports of an increase in crime and illness in the days running up to a full moon, it is also considered a time to make positive changes in your life, so if you are doing anything such as signing a contract, starting a new job or setting up in business, you will have greater success if you do this during a full moon.

The Waning Moon

The waning moon looks like it is diminishing and casts what looks like a C shape in the sky. It enters this phase from about three to 10 days after the full moon. When the moon is waning it is the ideal time to banish things from your life. Whether you want to get rid of an unsuitable partner, break a habit such as smoking, banish illness, or lose weight, then this is the time to do it. Witches use the waning moon to perform spells to get rid of anything in their life that is not doing them any good.

The New Moon

When you can't actually see the moon in the sky it doesn't mean that it's not there – it is. It's just not visible to us because there is no reflection from the sun during this phase. The new moon is said to be the time for new beginnings, so if you are looking for a new relationship, a new home, or even a whole new life, then this is the ideal time to do it.

If for example you wanted to lose weight, you could use the waning moon to banish your cravings for unsuitable food and then start your new diet during the new moon.

If you follow the phases of the moon, you will soon notice that you can in fact create your own destiny. By examining the patterns in your life against the moon phases, you will soon begin to see why your latest diet has failed again, or why you keep attracting the wrong partner. If you check the moon phase before you commit yourself to any major decision in your life and plan it so that it falls within the right moon phase, you will soon notice that you are more successful in your plans.

Moon Lore

- It is said that if a family member dies on the day of a new moon, 3 more deaths will follow.
- Many consider it unlucky to point at the moon.
- People born under a full-moon phase live lucky lives – check a moon calendar to see if you are one of them!
- It is said to be unlucky to marry on a waning moon.
- In England, France, Italy and Greece, the moon is considered to be a lady. In many other countries it is considered to be male.
- Don't get your hair cut on a Friday that falls on a new moon as it won't look like you expected!
- Medical staff report that women who have previously had children on a full moon are more likely to give birth to subsequent children on a full moon.

- More visits to GPs are made during the full moon and people who suffer from epileptic fits have more seizures during this time.
- In 1824 The Lunacy Act was written which stated that people were more likely to go mad during the full moon.
- Arson attacks rise by 100% at a full moon.
- Cutting or filing your fingernails on a Friday night when the moon is full is said to make them grow healthy and strong.
- If there are two new or full moons in the same month it predicts bad weather – this was recently evident in June of 2007 when we had the bad floods.
- It is said that if wood is cut during a new moon it will be hard to split. If it is cut during a full moon it will be easy to split.
- Grass crops should be sown at a full moon. Hay dries quicker if it is.
- In Wales, fishermen avoid seeing the moon reflecting on the water when heading off to sea, believing it to be bad luck.
- The moon is about 250,000 miles from earth.
- The moon appears to change shape, but what we actually see is the moon lit up by the light from the sun.
- Witches and Pagans cast their spells in accordance with the cycles of the moon.

Table of moon phases of when to do certain things

Full Moon	Waning Moon	New Moon	Waxing Moon
Sign new contracts	Quit a habit	View a new house	Start eating healthily
Start a new job	Lose weight	Buy a new house	Visit a casino
Set up a business	Banish illness	Make new friends	Find new friends
Join a club	Dump a partner	Arrange an interview	Attend an interview
Go travelling	Banish debt	Start a new diet	Write letters

Traditional Superstitions

Folklore is packed with superstitions. Here are just a few common ones and how they came about...

Walking Under Ladders
The superstition of avoiding walking under ladders has nothing to do with avoiding an accident with a falling pot of paint, but more to do with evading the wrath of the gods. This superstition comes from the shape a leaning ladder forms with the wall and the ground. It is believed that the triangle signals the Holy Trinity or a sacred space which should not be entered. If you happen to find yourself under a ladder, you should cross your fingers to weaken the power of the gods.

Ridding a Wart
There are many superstitions to get rid of a whole host of minor ailments such as warts. One such ancient superstition involves an apple and a pig. By rubbing the wart with a peeled apple and giving it to a pig it is thought that the pig will carry the wart back to its sty. However, it is also considered unlucky to have a pig cross your path, so bear this in mind if you're planning to rid your wart to a pig.

A Black Cat Crossing Your Path
A black cat crossing your path is lucky or unlucky, depending on where you live. Norse legend tells of a witch called Freya whose chariot was pulled by six black cats that were possessed by the Devil. This led to the belief that black cats were witches' familiars and if one crossed your path, the Devil was watching you. However, if you were to believe Egyptian mythology, the black cat is considered to be a sacred animal as depicted by Bast, the daughter of Isis. It is commonly believed today that if a black cat

walks towards you, you will have good fortune. If it walks away, it will take luck away with it.

Upstairs, Downstairs

It is said to be very unlucky to pass anyone on the stairs and if you must, do so with your fingers crossed. The stairs were originally thought to symbolise ascending to the gods. Should you pass another person on a staircase, it would make them angry. Added to this, early staircases were very narrow, so people passing were open to attack from behind. However, it's good to trip on a staircase. This is said to be a good omen and indicates a wedding will take place soon.

Under my Umbrella

It may have done Rihanna no harm, but opening an umbrella inside is considered by many to be a sign of bad luck. This superstition comes from the idea that an umbrella protects against the storms of life. If you open one in your home, it is thought that the household guardian spirits will think you are not grateful for their protection and they will leave. It was believed that everyone in the house would then be cursed without the spirit protection.

Knock on Wood

Many people today still knock on wood when they want something good to happen, but few know why they do it. The ancient druids believed that trees were the home to gods and lucky sprites that protected the forests. By knocking once on a tree and making a wish it was thought that the sprites would grant the wish. By knocking a second time it was considered a way of saying thank you.

Palmistry

Every gypsy you will ever come across will know all about palmistry. It's in their genes and usually taught at a very young age. The correct term for palmistry is chiromancy, meaning 'hand divination' in Greek.

Palmistry originally came from the Far East, but is practiced all over the world and is still used today. The lines on our hands change as we grow older. If you look at a baby's palm, you will see that their hands have very few lines on them. This is because as we grow and experience life, the lines on our palms reflect this. If we are shown encouragement from whoever is caring for us, this will reflect in the lines in our palms.

The older we get and the more experience we have in life also shows up in our palms. We may start out as a trusting soul, but life circumstances could teach us to be more careful in future and the lines on our palms will change to show our emotional changes.

In Japan, palm reading is taken so seriously that Japanese folk are having operations on their palms to change the lines on their hands to more favourable ones, such as their life and fate lines.

The great thing about learning palmistry is that it's a subject that intrigues most people and makes for a terrific ice-breaker at a party! The other great thing is that the more you practice reading people's palms, the better you will become at it. For example; a typical manual worker's palm will be hard to the touch and they generally have large fingers, but you may discover that such a palm on closer inspection reveals a lot of creative and emotional lines. This would suggest that although the person works in a manual environment, they are very artistic or creative, but haven't as yet been able to follow their dream path.

So let's get started on the basics of palm reading...

Hand shapes

As with all parts of our body, hands come in all shapes and sizes. Below are the main hand shapes that you will come across:

Square

Hands that are broad and square, with thick fingers and thumbs suggest this person has a no-nonsense approach to life. A spade's a spade and they are practical hard workers who prefer the outdoors to an office. The skin on square hands is usually thick in texture and the majority of manual workers have hands like these.

Long

Long and slender hands suggest this person is naturally curious about life, but can be a bit airy-fairy at times. If you drew around the hand, it would be almost rectangle. People with long and slender hands can be very imaginative and are often writers. They are also very social people, but can seem a little aloof when you first meet them.

Short

Although this palm usually has long fingers, the actual palm length is short. This hand suggests a very energetic person who gets bored easily. They have to be on the go all the time. The skin on these hands is usually soft and subtle.

Equal

This sort of palm looks like an equally proportioned hand. The fingers are neither too long nor too short and suggest an artistic person with a high IQ. They are in tune with their feelings and emotions and often those of others. They don't cope well in a crisis though.

Hand shapes are not always just one category though. Sometimes you will come across a palm that is almost in equal proportions but for having long fingers. This would suggest that although they are intelligent, they will get bored easily if their minds are not occupied. Palm reading is a bit like peeling back the layers of an old painting. The hand shapes give you a glimpse of what sort of person you are dealing with, but the lines will tell you for certain what they are really like!

The Major Palm Lines

The major lines on a palm get to the truth of who you are dealing with. Not everyone will have every major line on their hand and some may be more detailed than others, so don't worry if you can't find a specific line on your palm! When reading palms, there is some debate as to whether you should read the left palm, the right or both. Palmist students are taught to read both hands. A right-handed person's hand will be their active hand and their left hand will be their passive hand. The passive hand is the one where inherited traits and characteristics will be shown, whereas the active hand will show learned behaviours.

The Life Line

This line begins at the top of the thumb and goes all the way down to the bottom in a half circle or crescent moon shape. Contrary to popular belief it does not indicate how long your life will be and calling it the life line is a bit misleading, I think. The life line shows the state of a person's health and their enthusiasm for life. A line that breaks and rejoins suggests that the person will take a career change, or there will be a change in their love life. If the life line forks at some point, it suggests that the person will travel or will move away for a while in search of something different.

A faint life line can suggest that the person is low in energy and stamina and a short life line suggests that the person is easily influenced by others and needs to stand up for herself a bit more.

Life lines that start high on the palm indicate that this person is a born leader and very confident.

The Head Line

The head line is the one that starts near to the top of the life line and runs horizontally (often in a downwards direction) across the palm. The head line is the line that tells us all about the person's way of thinking, their intelligence and emotions. A long head line suggests a person's thirst for knowledge and shows someone who is a deep thinker and perhaps overanalyses things a lot.

If the head line is curvy, it suggests you have a good imagination. A straight line shows someone who is more logical in their thinking. If the head line is very long, it highlights that the person it belongs to has a long memory and tends to hold a grudge. A short line suggests a more forgiving person.

If the head line is broken it can suggest that you will have some important decisions to make. This is often seen when a person is deciding whether or not to go to university and you will notice that the line often corrects itself once a decision has been made. Crosses throughout the head line also suggest important decisions will have to be made.

The Heart Line

This line is found running across the top of the palm starting from just below the index finger and finishing just below the little finger. This line shows just how sensitive a person is and whether they are materialistic or emotional in love.

When this line is low on the palm, it shows that the person's heart rules their head. The straighter the line, the more the other person will keep their emotions to themselves. If it is curvy, it suggests that they will happily tell you all about their love lives whether you want to hear it or not!

If the heart line starts at the index finger, it means that your love life will be content. If it starts at the middle finger, you may have to deal with a selfish lover.

The Fate Line

Not everyone will have a fate line on their palm. If you remember, I mentioned that children often don't develop this line until they are in their teens and have an idea of where their life is taking them.

The fate line shows you what fate has in store for you, in particular in your career. This line runs down the centre of your palm. If it starts next to the life line then you are a self-made person, who will know early on in life what you want to do and achieve. If your fate line begins on the base of your thumb, it suggests that family support will be important to you.

If there are any breaks in your fate line, it suggests that you will change career at some point in your life. If this line starts at the bottom of your palm, it indicates that you are a born entertainer and you could find yourself in the public eye.

Minor Lines

Marriage Lines

The lines that you see just below the little finger are your marriage lines. Light lines are romances. Stronger, more defined lines suggest marriage and the longer the marriage lines, the longer the marriage will be. If you have a fork at the start of your marriage line, it means that you will get married but only after a long engagement. If there is a fork at the end of the marriage line, it suggests the marriage won't last.

Children Lines

The child lines are small vertical lines that sit on top of, or cross, the relationship lines. In old-fashioned palmistry, a strong line was supposed to represent a boy and a weak line a girl. Some palmists say a straight line is a boy and a slanted line is a girl.

These days, most palmistry experts agree that the marriage lines and child lines are not reliable with regard to the number of relationships/children.

Health

You can tell a lot about a person's health by looking at their hands:

Nails

It's not just the lines on your hands that can give you an indication of health problems. Your nails hold vital clues as to the wellbeing of your body and are worth looking at. Medical researchers discovered a link between the condition of a person's fingernails and their wellbeing and this practice is still highly regarded in medicine today.

Pale Nails

Pale/white nails can indicate that a person is anaemic and requires more iron in their diet. Another indication of anaemia is when the nails are slightly convex in their shape.

Blue Finger Tips

Blue finger tips or mauve nails suggest that the person has heart or circulation problems. If the nails are blue and raised this suggests that the person could have heart or lung disease.

Spotty Nails

If you notice white spots on your nails this can indicate that you are run down and lacking in some essential vitamins. This is often seen in teenagers or people working night shifts due to their disturbed sleeping patterns.

Ridges on the Nails

Ridges running horizontally across the nail suggest an emotional trauma; for example, an accident or an operation. If there are many ridges it indicates a nervous disposition such as anxiety, stress or early signs of depression. Meditation, yoga or Reiki will rectify this.

Indentations

Small indentations on the nails suggest skin diseases such as psoriasis, alopecia and eczema. If the nails are discoloured and indented at the top this suggests there is a build up of acid in the body leading to possible kidney problems.

Unusual Colours

If your nails are red in colour this can indicate high blood pressure. If the nail is a light purple it suggests low blood pressure or heart and lung problems. Half moons on the nails suggest a healthy balance.

Short Nails

Nails that are naturally short (not bitten) can suggest that the person could have problems with their stomach, bladder, kidneys or pancreas.

HAND COLOUR

The colour of our hands can give a clear indication as to how healthy we are:

- White hands indicate a lack of circulation and possibly an iron deficiency.
- Pink hands are usually a sign that the person is in good health.
- Red hands indicate a person with high blood pressure.
- Blue hands suggest someone who has bad circulation of

the blood supply.

- Yellow hands suggest someone who is suffering with jaundice.
- Hot hands which are also moist can suggest an overactive thyroid.
- Cold hands suggest someone with anaemia or an iron deficiency.

HANDS CHANGE

No one has the perfect palm so don't worry if you spot something that indicates a warning sign, it is just that – a forewarning. If you are at all concerned you are advised to visit your GP and get it checked out. The lines and marks on your hands don't stay the same. As you change and grow so too do your hands. If you notice a change in your hands such as an unusual marking indicating that you are anaemic and you get treatment you will notice that the original markings on your palm will disappear as you get better.

Put a Ring on It

Where a person chooses to wear a ring tells you a lot about them as a person:

The Thumb

Someone who wears a ring on their thumb highlights that they are transforming into someone new. It's almost as if they are saying, I am no longer conforming to what other's expect of me.

The Middle Finger

Wearing a ring on your middle finger suggests that the person wants to be taken seriously in life. The middle finger is usually the longest digit and wearing a ring on this particular finger shows that this person is worried about what other people think about them.

The Index Finger

Wearing a ring on your index finger shows that you are a bit low in self-esteem, but wish you could be stronger. People who wear a ring on this finger wish they were more assertive and tend to think of great comebacks after the event.

The Ring Finger

By tradition this finger is reserved for engagement or wedding rings, but many single people still wear a ring on this finger. This is a sign of wanting to appear attractive to the opposite sex. This is also a sign of a passionate person.

The Little Finger

Wearing a ring on the little finger suggests someone who can easily tell a white lie. It also shows this person has a problem expressing their feelings and can appear emotionally detached.

Romany gypsies traditionally wear a lot of jewellery, including many rings. Part of the reason for this is for decoration, but also because they used to travel around a lot; they would invest their money into gold jewellery, which was easier (and safer) to carry around than to carry money.

Well, we have come to the end of the book now and have covered a lot of subjects along the way. Whether you prefer Tarot reading to numerology, Runes to palmistry, you should have a general idea of how each divination system works, enough for you to be able to give accurate readings to other people.

With any divination system, it's important to practice as much as you can and use your intuition, because this is rarely ever wrong. It's when we start questioning that little voice inside our head that we start to doubt our original thoughts, so always go with your first instincts whenever you do a reading.

This book is designed to give you the basics of several different fortune-telling techniques. There are many more books out there that focus solely on one specific form of divination, so if you find you are drawn to one particular subject then I would encourage you to study that subject in more detail.

Thank you for choosing this book!

Soul Rocks is a fresh list that takes the search for soul and spirit mainstream. Chick-lit, young adult, cult, fashionable fiction & non-fiction with a fierce twist.